SUPERCARS

AND OTHER MEGA MACHINES

PAUL HARRISON

Arcturus

ARCTURUS

This edition published in 2014 by Arcturus Publishing Limited
26/27 Bickels Yard, 151–153 Bermondsey Street,
London SE1 3HA

Written by Paul Harrison
Edited by Joe Harris, Joe Fullman, and Frances Evans
Designed by sprout.uk.com, Matt Pull, and Dynamo Limited

ISBN: 978-1-78404-213-4
CH004218US
Supplier 26, Date 0814, Print Run 3315

Printed in China

CONTENTS

INTRODUCTION

From sleek supercars and high-octane racers to amazing aquatic vehicles and super-cool copters, this book explores some of the fastest, most powerful, and most formidable vehicles ever created. They are illustrated with high-quality photographs, with close ups to show special features, and tons of stats and facts. So what are you waiting for? Start your engines, and roar into action!

EXTREME
SUPER

What is an extreme supercar? It's a car, but not as we normally know it. The sleek vehicles featured in this chapter are faster, more expensive, and more eye-catching than any ordinary car you'll see driving along the street!

CARS

FERRARI 458 ITALIA

What makes the Ferrari 458 an extreme supercar and one of the world's most desirable cars? Drop-dead good looks help, plus it can reach amazing speeds. In fact, the 458 Italia is one of the best supercars that money can buy. It's easy to spot one—just look for the crowd of admirers standing around taking photos!

You don't get a lot of frills for your money. If you want GPS or to connect your iPod inside the 458 you have to pay extra! There may not be many frills, but there are still plenty of thrills.

There is an open-top version of this car, too, called the 458 Spider. Even though it doesn't have a roof, it's actually more expensive than the Italia!

Owners can choose many different options for their car. They can even choose how wide they would like the stitching on the seats to be.

Ferrari has a proud car racing history, which is why its cars are traditionally red. This was the color of Italian racing cars and Ferrari has kept the color ever since.

Air vents near the front lights help to cool the brakes.

The 458 is known as a "baby Ferrari," which means it is one of the smaller cars made by the company. It doesn't make it any less super though—it's actually faster than some of the larger Ferraris! And at a cost of $230,000 there's nothing babyish about its price tag.

The horse logo was first used in 1923 as a tribute to Francesco Barraca. He was an Italian World War I air force hero who used the prancing horse on his plane.

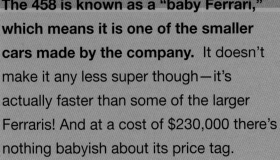

SUPER STATS

FERRARI 458 ITALIA
TOP SPEED: 202 mph (325 km/h)
0–60 mph (0–97 km/h): 3.4 seconds
FUEL ECONOMY (COMBINED): 20.6 mpg
HORSEPOWER: 562 bhp
LENGTH: 178.2 in (4,527 mm)
WIDTH: 76.3 in (1,937 mm)
HEIGHT: 47.8 in (1,213 mm)
MADE IN: Italy
PRICE: $230,000

PORSCHE 911
CARRERA 4S

The Porsche 911 Carrera 4S is incredible—even by supercar standards—and that's because it's a supercar you can use every day. This might not sound too amazing, but usually when designers make a supercar they think about its looks first and then how useful it is. That's not the case with the 911, though—it's a dream to drive and there's even space for a suitcase. Very few supercars can compete with that.

Most of the car's body panels are made from aluminum, which is strong but very light. The lighter the car is, the faster it can go!

The first designs for the 911 were drawn by Ferdinand Porsche—the same man who designed the original Volkswagen Beetle!

The Carrera 4S version of the 911 is unusual for a Porsche as the engine power goes to all four wheels instead of just the rear wheels. This is a truly speedy 4x4!

Four-wheel drive helps the car to grip the road surface in wet conditions.

The driver can alter any aspect of the car's performance. Buttons adjust everything, from the transmission and how the car handles to the noise the exhaust makes.

The 911 is one of the longest lasting supercar models ever! The first 911 rolled off the production lines in 1963 and surprisingly the car's shape hasn't changed very much at all—perhaps the designers thought they'd got it right the first time.

Unlike most cars, the 911 has its engine at the back. This could cause the car to swing out on tight bends. However, the 911's excellent grip stops this from happening.

The designers of the Porsche 911 caused an outcry among fans when they decided to change the way the engine was cooled. They changed from air vents to a more standard water cooling method. That proves that this car is so super, no one wants anything to be changed!

SUPER STATS

PORSCHE 911 CARRERA 4S
TOP SPEED: 185 mph (299 km/h)
0–60 mph (0–97 km/h) : 4.5 seconds
FUEL ECONOMY (COMBINED): 28.5 mpg
HORSEPOWER: 400 bhp
LENGTH: 176.8 in (4,491 mm)
WIDTH: 72.9 in (1,852 mm)
HEIGHT: 51.0 in (1,296 mm)
MADE IN: Germany
PRICE: $85,000

LAMBORGHINI AVENTADOR

The Lamborghini Aventador is the ultimate supercar because it combines stunning good looks with powerful speed. It's hugely wide and incredibly low. And the noise from its massive V12 engine can be heard from the other end of town. This shouldn't bother Aventador owners though—if you drive a car like this, you probably enjoy all the attention.

Like most supercars, the Aventador only has two seats, which is bad news if you need to give more than one person a lift.

The Aventador is blisteringly quick—so fast, in fact, that the Dubai police force has bought one as a specialist pursuit vehicle. That should mean they can catch almost anyone else on the road. It also means they've got the coolest police car around.

The body of the Aventador is made from carbon fiber. Apart from being strong and light it will also never rust.

The body needs to be strong to stop it from twisting when the car goes around corners.

The Aventador has what are called "scissor doors." This describes the way they swing up and down to open and close.

Although famous for its supercars, Lamborghini actually started out by making tractors! The owner, Ferruccio Lamborghini, felt he had been insulted by the Ferrari car company. So he vowed to build cars that would put Ferrari in the shade. The Aventador is the latest in a long line of amazing cars that resulted from Ferruccio's decision.

Although the Aventador uses fuel like it's going out of fashion, it does try to be green (honestly!). Every time you stop, the engine switches off to save gas. Then it starts again in just 180 milliseconds when you want to move on.

SUPER STATS

LAMBORGHINI AVENTADOR
TOP SPEED: 217 mph (350 km/h)
0–60 mph (0–97 km/h) : 2.9 seconds
FUEL ECONOMY (COMBINED): 16.4 mpg
HORSEPOWER: 700 bhp
LENGTH: 188.2 in (4,780 mm)
WIDTH: 89.2 in (2,265 mm)
HEIGHT: 44.7 in (1,136 mm)
MADE IN: Italy
PRICE: $390,000

ASTON MARTIN
V12 ZAGATO

Aston Martin, the creator of James Bond's car of choice, has been voted the coolest brand in the world six times since 2000! Its cars don't get any cooler than the V12 Zagato. This so-cool-it's-ice-cold car is made by Aston Martin and Italian company Zagato. The V12 proves these companies know how to make a beautiful supercar.

Aston Martin invented four new color shades which are used on the Zagato and no other car.

It takes 100 hours to paint each car!

Zagato is a "coachbuilder," which means that it makes the bodies of cars for different companies. Zagato and Aston Martin have worked together for 50 years to make limited editions of Aston Martin cars.

Aston Martin will only make 101 of these cars, so they are bound to become collector's items.

The Zagato isn't really a new car at all. It's basically an Aston Martin Vanquish with a new body on top. And with a bigger price tag—it's more than $130,000 more expensive than a Vanquish!

When designing the car, Aston Martin tried out an early model on the racetrack in a genuine competitive race—and won.

SUPER STATS

ASTON MARTIN V 12 ZAGATO
TOP SPEED: 190 mph (305 km/h)
0–60 mph (0–97 km/h) : 4.2 seconds
FUEL ECONOMY (COMBINED): 17.3 mpg
HORSEPOWER: 510 bhp
LENGTH: 172.6 in (4,385 mm)
WIDTH: 79.6 in (2,022 mm)
HEIGHT: 49.2 in (1,250 mm)
MADE IN: Great Britain
PRICE: $450,000

MORGAN AEROMAX

The Morgan Aero Coupe looks as though it belongs on a 1930s film set, but it's actually one of today's most interesting supercars. It has a traditional design but uses very modern technology. The Aero Coupe might have jaw-dropping looks and blistering speed, but it's made slowly and with care—which makes it all the more desirable.

The sporty looking Aero Coupe is based on a Morgan racing car called the GT3 Aero.

Morgan doesn't make its own engines. The engine in the Aero Coupe comes from the German car makers BMW.

The interior of the car is trimmed with a hardwood called ash. This can be hand polished into different colors.

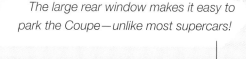

The large rear window makes it easy to park the Coupe—unlike most supercars!

Morgan cars might have modern-day technology, but they also use traditional carmaking techniques. For example, the cars are hand built and customers can choose different colors and interiors to make their car unique. This all takes time, though—so if you want one, you'd better be prepared to wait.

Morgan makes other cars that look even more old-fashioned than the Aero Coupe!

Designers used high-tech super formed aluminum panels for the entire body.

The car frame is made from aluminum too, as Morgan believes it gives a combination of lightness and strength.

SUPER STATS

MORGAN AERO COUPE
TOP SPEED: 170 mph (273 km/h)
0–60 mph (0–97 km/h) : 4.5 seconds
FUEL ECONOMY (COMBINED): 23 mpg
HORSEPOWER: 315 bhp
LENGTH: 163 in (4,147 mm)
WIDTH: 68.9 in (1,751 mm)
HEIGHT: 49.1 in (1,248 mm)
MADE IN: Great Britain
PRICE: $165,000

MCLAREN F1

The ultimate supercar combines showstopping good looks with incredible speed. The McLaren F1 ticks both those boxes. McLaren runs a highly successful Formula 1 racing team, so it's no surprise to learn that when the company made a road car called the F1, it was the fastest on the market. Twenty years later, it's still one of the fastest cars on the road and it's still good-looking enough to draw a crowd.

It took four years to design and build the F1.

The F1's engine bay was lined with gold foil because it reflected more of the heat produced by the V12 engine than any other material.

To keep the car's weight down, even the toolkit is made from titanium, a metal that is only half as heavy as steel.

The wheels are made from a magnesium alloy—McLaren's choice for strength and lightness.

Other supercars may have beaten the F1's record of world's fastest road car, but it's still one of the most desirable cars around. Only 64 of the road versions were ever made, so getting hold of one can be tricky. When one does come up for sale, they aren't cheap. In 2012, an F1 was sold at auction for a staggering $5 million!

Although the F1 was a highly advanced car, it didn't have ABS, traction control, or even power steering—all available on normal family cars.

Strangely, the F1 has three seats—there's one in the middle up front for the driver and two behind for passengers. It's a bit like the world's fastest taxi!

SUPER STATS

MCLAREN F1
TOP SPEED: 240 mph (386 km/h)
0–60 mph (0–97 km/h) : 3.2 seconds
FUEL ECONOMY (COMBINED): 15.2 mpg
HORSEPOWER: 620 bhp
LENGTH: 168.8 in (4,288 mm)
WIDTH: 71.7 in (1,820 mm)
HEIGHT: 45.2 in (1,149 mm)
MADE IN: Great Britain
PRICE: $1 million when new; $5 million + at auction

PAGANI HUAYRA

Supercars are meant to be exclusive—they're not everyday cars after all. Being exclusive also means that they're usually very expensive. But there aren't many that cost as much as the Pagani Huayra. At nearly $1.4 million, the Huayra is eye-wateringly expensive, but you do get an amazing car for your cash.

The weight of the car is almost perfectly balanced between the front and the back of the car. This makes for a car that handles excellently.

Every bolt in the Huayra is made from titanium and is stamped with the car company's name.

More than 4,000 different parts make up the Huayra—and that doesn't include the engine or transmission.

There are flaps that pop up at the front and back of the car. These help to press the car to the road and give the Huayra extra grip—especially round corners.

Pagani is a small Italian company— big enough to build brilliant cars, but not big enough to build everything itself. This means that it works with other companies that make parts such as the brakes, the engine, and the exhaust system. Of course, these are all made to the highest standard demanded by Pagani.

When the driver applies the brakes the special flaps pop up to help slow the car down. These flaps, called air brakes, are also used by aircraft!

No expense has been spared. Even the clocks inside the Huayra are made by Rolex, the luxury watch maker.

SUPER STATS

PAGANI HUAYRA
TOP SPEED: 225 mph (362 km/h)
0–60 mph (0–97 km/h) : 3.3 seconds
FUEL ECONOMY (COMBINED): 18.8 mpg
HORSEPOWER: 720 bhp
LENGTH: 181.3 in (4,605 mm)
WIDTH: 80.2 in (2,036 mm)
HEIGHT: 46.0 in (1,169 mm)
MADE IN: Italy
PRICE: $1.4 million

FISKER KARMA

The Fisker Karma is a different sort of supercar. For a start, it's got real room for rear passengers and four doors so they can get in and out easily. But the most amazing thing about the Karma is that it is partly powered by electricity, not just gasoline. So it's a green supercar—you don't see many of those around!

The roof doubles as a solar panel, which generates enough electricity to power all the lighting and extends the distance, or range, that the car is able to travel.

The headlights use LED bulbs, which are bright and don't use much electricity.

Celebrities such as Usher and Justin Bieber own Fisker Karmas.

The biggest problem with electric cars is that they have a short range. If you drive too far, then the batteries run flat and you come to a stop. The Karma gets around this problem by having two engines in one. You can drive just using the electric motor, or with both gasoline and electricity powering the car.

The Karma was designed by the same man who created the Aston Martin Vantage and the BMW Z8.

Electric cars don't make any sound, so the Karma makes a fake engine noise to warn people that it is approaching.

The only downside of the Karma is that having two power supplies makes it very heavy. However, that doesn't seem to affect the car's performance too much!

Some of the wood used to make the dashboard and doors look great is around 300 years old. What's more, the trees it came from were found sunk on the bottom of Lake Michigan!

SUPER STATS

FISKER KARMA
201 KM/H (125 MPH)
TOP SPEED: 125 mph (201 km/h)
0–60 mph (0–97 km/h) : 6.3 seconds
FUEL ECONOMY (COMBINED): Not available
HORSEPOWER: 260 bhp
LENGTH: 196.8 in (4,998 mm)
WIDTH: 84.0 in (2,133 mm)
HEIGHT: 52.4 in (1,330 mm)
MADE IN: USA
PRICE: $144,000

BLOODHOUND SSC

If a supercar is meant to be super-quick and super-rare, then Bloodhound SSC must be the most super of them all. Not only is it aiming to be the fastest car of all time, it's also one of a kind— and you don't get any more rare than that!

Bloodhound doesn't have just one engine—it has three! A jet engine gets it going, a rocket engine takes it up to top speed, and a race car engine keeps the power coming to the fuel pumps.

The jet engine is normally found on Eurofighter Typhoon airplanes.

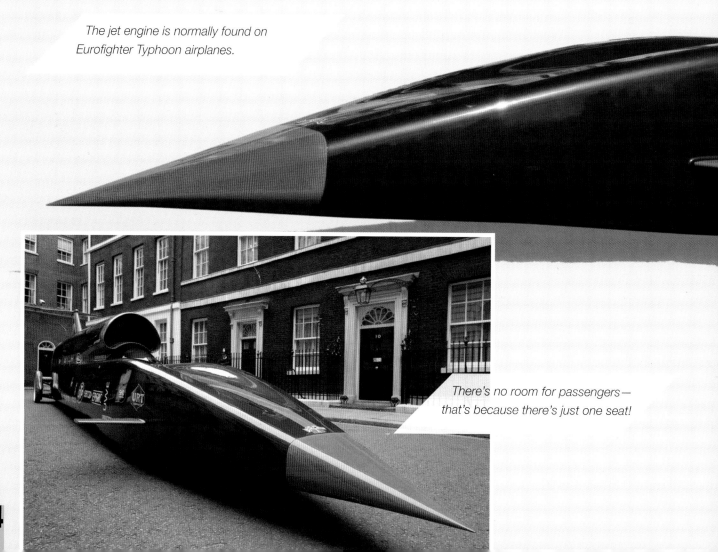

There's no room for passengers— that's because there's just one seat!

The letters SSC in Bloodhound's name stand for "supersonic car." That's because Bloodhound has been designed to travel faster than the speed of sound. The speed at which sound travels depends on your altitude, but at ground level it measures 767 mph (1,235 km/h). Bloodhound aims to smash that figure and hit speeds of over 1,000 mph (1,609 km/h)!

The car will be driven by a jet fighter pilot called Andy Green. He also drove the car that holds the current land speed record, Thrust SSC.

Normal tires on the wheels would fall apart at supersonic speeds. Instead, the wheels are made from solid aluminum.

Bloodhound will be traveling so quickly it will need three different types of brakes. It has normal wheel brakes, flaps that rise up called air brakes (which aircraft use), and parachutes.

The tall fin at the back helps keep the car pointing straight ahead.

SUPER STATS

BLOODHOUND SSC

TOP SPEED: More than 1,000 mph (more than 1,600 km/h)

0–60 mph (0–97 km/h) : Unknown

FUEL ECONOMY (COMBINED): Not available

HORSEPOWER: 135,000 bhp

LENGTH: 530.3 in (13,470 mm)

WIDTH: 74.8 in (1,900 mm)

HEIGHT: 118.1 in (3,000 mm)

MADE IN: Great Britain

PRICE: Not for sale

NOBLE M600

The Noble M600 is a rarity—a top level supercar that's not made by a gigantic car company. It is built by a small team of around twenty people on an industrial park in Britain. The M600 might be a David against the Goliaths of the supercar world, but it does something different to set itself apart from its richer cousins.

The body is made of carbon fiber, which is very strong and light.

There are three different settings that alter the way the car handles. The driver can choose road, sport, or race. Race is the fastest and road is the most comfortable.

The unique attraction of the M600 is that it's a really basic car—it's stripped back to the bare essentials. Other supercars have loads of fancy gizmos like paddle shift gears, electronic stability control, and anti-lock brakes. The M600 ignores all of these. The idea is that the more basic the car is, the more the driver feels like they are involved with the ride— and plenty of people agree with that idea.

Each car has its own number printed on the dashboard and the names of the people who built it engraved on the door sill.

Japanese firm Yamaha makes the engine. The same one was used in a Volvo SUV— but this wasn't as fast as the Noble!

SUPER STATS

NOBLE M600
TOP SPEED: 225 mph (362 km/h)
0–60 mph (0–97 km/h) : 3.5 seconds
FUEL ECONOMY (COMBINED): 18 mpg
HORSEPOWER: 650 bhp
LENGTH: 171.6 in (4,360 mm)
WIDTH: 75.2 in (1,910 mm)
HEIGHT: 44.8 in (1,140 mm)
MADE IN: Great Britain
PRICE: $330,000

MERCEDES SLR STIRLING MOSS

The Mercedes SLR Stirling Moss looks like a racing car from the 1950s and that's entirely deliberate. Mercedes has a proud tradition of building racing cars. This extreme supercar is named for one of the company's most famous racing drivers. And just like the racing car, the SLR has race-winning performance figures too!

The body is made from carbon fiber.

The two air scoops behind the seats also act as roll bars, which protect the driver and passenger if the car should ever roll over.

An air brake on the boot lid lifts automatically to provide extra grip and slow the car down.

The SLR is meant to look similar to the Mercedes that Stirling Moss drove in the 1950s.

When there are no passengers a special cover, known as a tonneau cover, goes over the passenger seat.

There are four exhaust pipes, two on each side at the front of the car.

As well as being a supercar, the **Mercedes SLR Stirling Moss is super exclusive.** Apart from its amazing speed, it's also very rare. Just 75 of them were made and not just anyone could buy one. Not only is it staggeringly expensive but potential owners were hand-picked by Mercedes. The company decided that only existing owners of Mercedes SLR cars would be able to buy one!

This Mercedes is a more basic version of their SLR range, a more run-of-the-mill supercar—if such a thing exists!

You don't get a lot for your money. There's no stereo, GPS, roof, or even a windscreen, so you have to wear goggles when you drive it.

SUPER STATS

MERCEDES SLR STIRLING MOSS
TOP SPEED: 217 mph (349 km/h)
0–60 mph (0–97 km/h) : 3.5 seconds
FUEL ECONOMY (COMBINED): 8 mpg
HORSEPOWER: 641 bhp
LENGTH: 183.3 in (4,656 mm)
WIDTH: 75.1 in (1,908 mm)
HEIGHT: 50.4 in (1,281 mm)
MADE IN: Germany
PRICE: $1.1 million

SPYKER C8 AILERON

Countries such as Italy, Britain, and Germany are well known for making supercars. But Spyker makes some of the most unusual and exciting cars on the planet and the company comes from a country that is not as famous for motoring. Spyker is based in the Netherlands and its C8 Aileron shows that the Dutch can make a supercar as well as anyone else!

The Spyker has a "rear diffuser." This uses the air traveling under the car to pull the car more tightly to the road and improve handling.

The air inlets on the roof and on the sides of the car are shaped like jet engines.

The wheels are meant to look like the blades in a jet turbine engine.

Spyker cars are hand-built.

Spyker used to make aircraft back in the early days of plane flight... and you can tell. The gear lever rods are left open to view as in an early plane instead of being hidden away. It has an aircraft-style ignition (starter) switch. "Aileron" is the name given to a movable flap on the wing of an airplane and Spyker describes the place where the driver sits as the "cockpit" and it being under the "canopy" rather than the "cabin" and the "roof."

The body panels and frame are made from aluminum.

The Spyker logo on the front of the hood is an old-fashioned propeller. That's because Spyker made fighter planes during World War I.

Aileron owners can order matching luggage made especially for Spyker by luxury bag maker Louis Vuitton—but it costs an extra $29,400. Those are some expensive bags!

SUPER STATS

SPYKER C8 AILERON
TOP SPEED: 187 mph (300 km/h)
0–60 mph (0–97 km/h) : 4.5 seconds
FUEL ECONOMY (COMBINED): 17 mpg
HORSEPOWER: 400 bhp
LENGTH: 181.8 in (4,618 mm)
WIDTH: 76.9 in (1,953 mm)
HEIGHT: 50.0 in (1,270 mm)
MADE IN: Netherlands
PRICE: $320,000

FORD GT

It's a strange fact that some of the world's most expensive supercars have been made by some of the smallest companies. And some of the biggest brands don't really make much of an effort when it comes to supercars. Take the Ford motor company, for example—it's huge, but the only supercar it has made in the last forty years is the GT. It was worth the wait though!

The driver presses a red button on the dashboard to start the engine.

The original GT40 was a successful racing car for Ford.

Unlike most supercars, the GT is easy to drive at low speeds. Often, supercars feel heavy and are difficult to steer.

Inside, the GT is a mixture of metal and a lightweight plastic and fiberglass mix called Azdel composite. Motorhomes also use Azdel composite, which perhaps makes the GT feel less special than it should!

One of the problems of supercars is their ridiculous width. TV presenter Jeremy Clarkson discovered this to his cost when his GT got stuck on Hammersmith Bridge in London because it was too wide!

The fuel tank is in the middle of the car to try and spread the weight evenly and to protect the tank in a crash.

Big, wide tires provide lots of grip.

The GT looks very similar to Ford's only other supercar, the GT40, which it built after falling out with Ferrari. That's the second time Ferrari has annoyed someone so much they went off and built a Ferrari-beating car. You would think they would have learned from the first time!

SUPER STATS

FORD GT
TOP SPEED: 212 mph (341 km/h)
0–60 mph (0–97 km/h) : 3.7 seconds
FUEL ECONOMY (COMBINED): 14.6 mpg
HORSEPOWER: 550 bhp
LENGTH: 182.8 in (4,643 mm)
WIDTH: 76.9 in (1,953 mm)
HEIGHT: 44.3 in (1,125 mm)
MADE IN: USA
PRICE: $205,000

ARIEL ATOM 3.5

Supercar buyers expect their vehicles to be filled with cutting-edge technology and to be made from the world's most up-to-date materials. That's not quite the case with the Ariel Atom, though, where the idea seems to be that less is more. The Atom doesn't have a roof, windshield, doors, or even body panels!

This air intake at the back also protects the driver in a crash.

The atom uses a Honda i-VTEC engine. The Japanese firm has made more than 13 million of these engines and not one of them has failed!

The Atom has won competitions for the fastest car to accelerate from 0 to 100 mph (160 km/h) and to return to 0 mph (0 km/h).

Although driving an Atom is like driving a Formula 1 racing car unlike the racer, the Atom has a seat for a passenger.

The chassis of the car wraps around the driver and passenger to offer them some protection.

Ariel started out by making old-fashioned bicycles back in the late 1800s. Although these bikes look strange to us today, at the time they were actually racing bikes. Ariel has continued to make sports vehicles ever since, from early grand prix cars and motor bikes to their present model, the Atom 3.5.

Although the Atom's engine is quite small, the car is still really quick thanks to its super-light weight.

Owners can buy a windshield if they want one—but most don't bother.

SUPER STATS

ARIEL ATOM 3.5
TOP SPEED: 155 mph (249 km/h)
0–60 mph (0–97 km/h) : 2.7 seconds
FUEL ECONOMY (COMBINED): Not known
HORSEPOWER: 310 bhp
LENGTH: 134.2 in (3,410 mm)
WIDTH: 72.0 in (1,828 mm)
HEIGHT: 47.0 in (1,195 mm)
MADE IN: Great Britain
PRICE: $50,000

RACING SUPER

These racing supercars may all look different but they have certain things in common—they can all reach blistering speeds to win races!

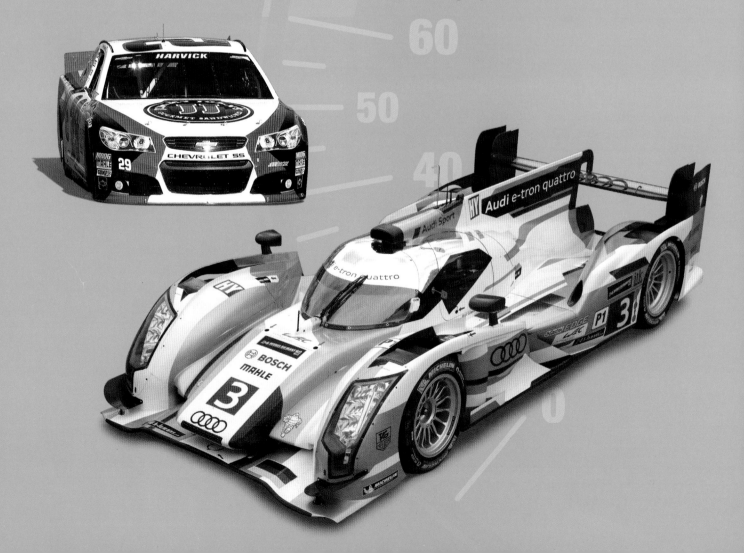

CARS

FERRARI F138

What makes a racing supercar super? Most racing cars are designed with one feature in mind—the ability to reach incredible speeds and win races! The Ferrari F138 is the most high-tech racing car on the track. This is the result of spending millions of dollars and many years on the car's design and testing.

The car's chassis is made from carbon fiber, which is both light and very strong. The carbon fiber is made in a honeycomb design to further reduce weight.

The large hole above the driver's head is an air intake. This diverts air toward the engine to keep it cool.

Flaps on the rear spoilers open and close to boost the car's speed.

Big tires give the car lots of grip on the race track.

The F138 was developed in a wind tunnel—a machine that shows designers how the air is flowing around the car. The more easily the air moves, the faster the car will go.

The Formula 1 World Championship is the world's most glamorous motor race series. To win it in 2013, Ferrari had to try to improve on the previous season's car. The rules about what teams can do to their cars change each season. So Ferrari designers were trying to get the best car they could while staying within the rules. The result was the F138.

The F138 has seven forward gears and one reverse gear.

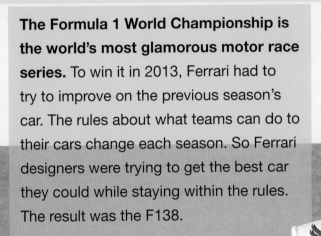

Spoilers on the front and back of the car use air to push the car to the track and give it extra grip.

SUPER STATS

FERRARI F138

TOP SPEED: Top secret but over 185 mph (300 km/h)

0–60 MPH (0–97 KM/H): Top secret but under 3 seconds

HORSEPOWER: Top secret

LENGTH: 178.9 in (4,545 mm)

WIDTH: 70.7 in (1,796 mm)

HEIGHT: 37.7 in (959 mm)

MADE IN: Italy

TOP FUEL FUNNY CAR

"Funny Cars" are no joke! They are a type of long, narrow drag racing car. And their lightning speeds and incredible acceleration are no laughing matter. In fact, in a straight race, a Funny Car would leave a Formula 1 car standing. That's because it is one of the fastest racing cars around.

The only cars faster than the Funny Cars are called Top Fuel Rails. These are longer, skinnier dragsters that have their engines at the back for better grip.

Many Funny Cars have no doors: instead the body of the car lifts up for the driver to get in.

The chassis is made from carbon fiber, a strong but lightweight material.

Massive back wheels are needed to provide enough grip and to cope with all the power the engine produces.

In a drag race, two dragsters race side by side over a short track. The race track measures 0.25 miles (0.4 km). There are different types of dragster, with the Top Fuel cars being the fastest. Typically, a Top Fuel car will finish the race in under 4 seconds!

Top Fuel cars don't use normal fuel but a mixture of gasoline and nitro methane. This fuel provides more power to the engine.

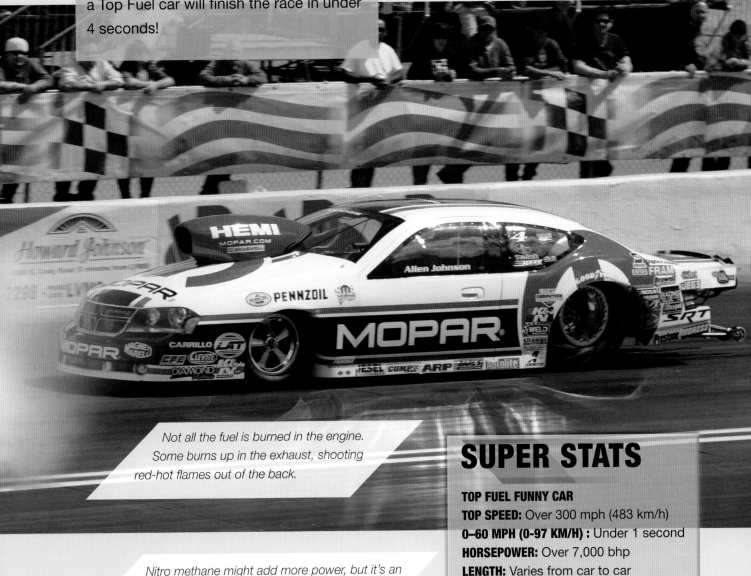

Not all the fuel is burned in the engine. Some burns up in the exhaust, shooting red-hot flames out of the back.

Nitro methane might add more power, but it's an expensive fuel to buy and dragsters use lots of it. A Top Fuel Funny Car can use around a gallon (3.6 l) in a second!

SUPER STATS

TOP FUEL FUNNY CAR
TOP SPEED: Over 300 mph (483 km/h)
0–60 MPH (0-97 KM/H) : Under 1 second
HORSEPOWER: Over 7,000 bhp
LENGTH: Varies from car to car
WIDTH: Varies from car to car
HEIGHT: Varies from car to car
MADE IN: Mainly USA

DRIFT RACING

Drift racing is different from most car racing. It's not about how fast you can go, but how good you are at skidding and spinning! The sport started in Japan in the 1960s and drifting competitions are now held worldwide. Models such as the Nissan 200SX and the Mazda RX-7 FD35 are considered to be some of the best drift racing cars.

Big clouds of smoke billow out from the back wheels as the car squeals and slides around the race track at lightning speed.

Drift racing cars usually have a rear-wheel drive, which means the power from the engine goes to the back wheels, not the front.

The engine in a drift racer is turbo-charged. This means it has a system that increases the power that the engine can produce, making the car faster.

Drift racing uses the skills of the driver to get the car into a controlled sideways slide as it travels around the race track. This may not be the fastest way of getting round the race track, but that's not the point. Instead, drivers get points for how well they control the slide. Cars often compete, one on one against each other in knockout tournaments.

A drift racer needs to control the car's accelerator, clutch, and brake pedals, as well as keeping an eye on the car's speed and steering.

Although there are drifting races all around the world, the sport is not controlled by the FIA (Federation Internationale de l'Automobile). The FIA is the organization that oversees most forms of professional motor sport.

SUPER STATS

DRIFT RACER (*The following stats relate to a Nissan 200SX*)
TOP SPEED: 146 mph (235 km/h)
0–60 MPH (0-97 KM/H) : 7 seconds
HORSEPOWER: 197 bhp
LENGTH: 178 in (4,521 mm)
WIDTH: 68.1 in (1,731 mm)
HEIGHT: 51 in (1,296 mm)
MADE IN: Japan

VOLKSWAGEN POLO R WRC

The Volkswagen Polo may be the hatchback car favored by grannies the world over, but it's unlikely your granny has ever been behind the wheel of the R WRC version of the Volkswagen Polo. That's because this is a top-level rally car, designed to compete in some of the toughest racing conditions going.

Unlike most cars involved in motor sports, rally cars are designed to seat two people—a driver and a navigator who directs the driver using a map. No GPS here!

The R WRC's engine is a lot more powerful than the one found in a standard Polo.

Unlike the road-going version of the Polo, the rally version has had its back seats taken out and a support cage built inside for protection in the event of a crash. And in rallying, the chances of a crash are particularly high.

A large spoiler at the back of the car helps use the air flowing over the car to push the Polo downward, helping it to find grip on slippery surfaces.

Bigger, stronger brakes are needed to slow the car more quickly—otherwise the Polo would end up wrapped around a tree or in a ditch.

Rally car races take place over a range of different road surfaces, varying from paved roads to gravel tracks to ice and snow. That's tough on any car, and to make it even harder the rules state that rally cars, such as the Polo, have to be based on models that the general public can buy. Imagine pulling out of your driveway in an R WRC!

The body of the car has to be specially reinforced to help it survive any hard knocks.

SUPER STATS

VOLKSWAGEN POLO R WRC
TOP SPEED: Around 125 mph (200 km/h)
0–60 MPH (0-97 KM/H) : Around 3.9 seconds
HORSEPOWER: 315 bhp
LENGTH: 156.5 in (3,976 mm)
WIDTH: 71.6 in (1,820 mm)
HEIGHT: 53.3 in (1,356 mm)
MADE IN: Germany

Rally cars may have small engines, but they can still reach speeds of around 125 mph (200 km/h).

PEUGEOT 208 T16

At first glance, the Peugeot 208 T16 looks just like any other rally car. But the T16 is a record-breaking racing machine, specially modified to take part in a unique type of race known as hill climbing. This Peugeot is super fast, super powerful, and super grippy—the ideal combination for conquering the unique conditions of hill climbing.

Speed is essential and it takes less than 2 seconds for the T16 to get from 0 mph to 60 mph (0–100 km/h)!

There are huge spoilers on the front and the back of the T16 to push the car down onto the road surface for extra grip.

The chassis is made from lightweight carbon fiber panels over a strong tubular steel frame.

The rear spoiler was originally designed for a car that was meant to compete in 24-hour races such as the famous Le Mans event.

Hill climbing is incredibly tough and the courses include steep uphill climbs as well as tight turns and hairpin bends. This means the Peugeot T16 has to be able to accelerate and decelerate quickly. It also needs to have excellent grip and road handling—and of course an excellent driver!

In 2013 the T16 won the famous Pikes Peak hill climb race in the USA in record-breaking time.

The T16's wheel arches are bigger than a standard 208 car to allow larger wheels to be used. Bigger wheels mean bigger tires and bigger tires give more grip.

The T16's brakes are made from a material called carbon ceramic. They are lighter and give better results than standard metal brakes.

SUPER STATS

PEUGEOT 208 T16
TOP SPEED: 149 mph (240 km/h)
0–60 MPH (0-97 KM/H) : 1.8 seconds
HORSEPOWER: 875 bhp
LENGTH: 177.2 in (4,500 mm)
WIDTH: 78.7 in (2,000 mm)
HEIGHT: 51.2 in (1,300 mm)
MADE IN: France

SANDRAIL

Sandrails are the ultimate "build-it-yourself" racing supercars. These ultra-light specialist racers are the Frankenstein's monsters of the car racing world. Built from bits and pieces of other cars and held together with some DIY welding, they may not sound great, but nothing beats a sandrail for blasting across sand dunes.

Sandrails have very few body panels, which keeps their weight down.

Large tires help to spread the weight of the car better than small tires and prevent the car sinking into soft sand.

Sandrails get their name from the fact that the cars look like they have been made from long pieces of steel—which in fact they have!

The rear tires have large, evenly spaced ridges, known as paddles, for extra grip on the slippery sand.

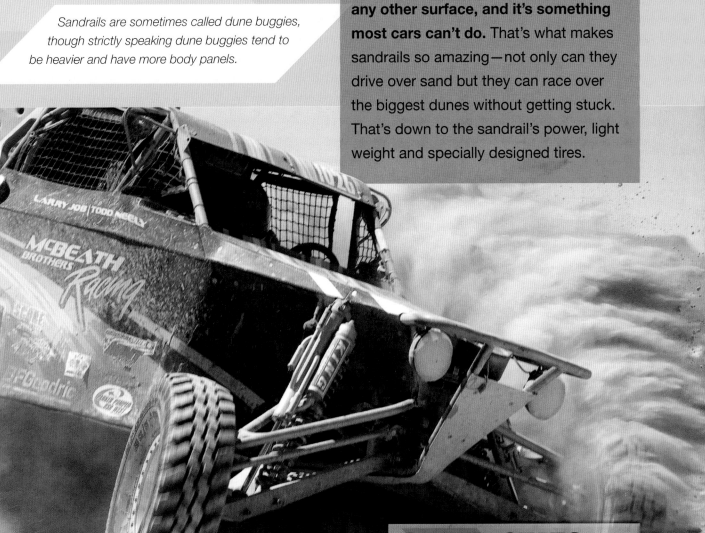

Sandrails are sometimes called dune buggies, though strictly speaking dune buggies tend to be heavier and have more body panels.

Driving on sand is unlike traveling on any other surface, and it's something most cars can't do. That's what makes sandrails so amazing—not only can they drive over sand but they can race over the biggest dunes without getting stuck. That's down to the sandrail's power, light weight and specially designed tires.

Sandrails work well in extreme muddy conditions, too!

SUPER STATS

SANDRAIL *(All figures are just a guide as each sandrail will be different)*
TOP SPEED: 70 mph (113 km/h)
0–60 MPH (0-97 KM/H): 7 seconds
HORSEPOWER: 68 bhp
LENGTH: 122 in (3,098 mm)
WIDTH: 84 in (2,134 mm)
HEIGHT: 60 in (1,524 mm)
MADE IN: USA

SUNSWIFT IV AND EVE

Imagine driving a car and never having to worry about fuel! Well, that dream is a reality with Sunswift IV. This supercar runs on the power of the Sun alone by converting energy from the Sun's rays into electricity that powers the car. As if this wasn't incredible enough, Sunswift IV is also a record breaker. It's the fastest solar-powered car on the planet!

The top, flat surface of the car is basically a large set of solar panels.

The Sunswift IV, nicknamed Ivy, has three narrow wheels. Big fat tires would cause more friction on the road which would slow the car down.

Sunswift IV is good for the environment because it doesn't cause any pollution. However, it's not good for passengers— there's only one seat!

The energy from the solar panels can be used to power the car or can be stored in a battery and used later.

For the last couple of decades there have been competitions to produce the best solar-powered cars. Generally the cars, like Sunswift, are built by students and scientists trying to beat records for either speed or distance. The latest addition from Sunswift, called eVe, aims to look more like a traditional car. It has four wheels and there's room for both a driver and a passenger!

Although the solar panels only generate enough power to boil a kettle, the Sunswift eVe is so well designed this is enough electricity to make the car move.

The body is made from lightweight carbon fiber.

Cowlings around the front wheels help to make the car more aerodynamic.

SUPER STATS

SUNSWIFT IV
TOP SPEED: 70 mph (115 km/h)
0–60 MPH (0-97 KM/H) : Not applicable
HORSEPOWER: Not applicable
LENGTH: 181 in (4,600 mm)
WIDTH: 70.8 in (1,800 mm)
HEIGHT: 70.8 in (1,800 mm)
MADE IN: USA

HONDA CIVIC NGTC

If you want extreme driving thrills from a run-of-the-mill family hatchback, then the Honda Civic NGTC is the car for you. This super-version of the family model takes part in the British Touring Car Championships and proves that big surprises—and big performances—can come in small packages!

The key to successful racing is speed, so the engine is more than twice as powerful as a standard Honda Civic—and accelerates twice as fast.

The engine costs around $40,000— more than enough to buy a brand new version of a normal Honda Civic, but cheap by motor racing standards.

A steel safety cage inside the car protects the driver in the event of a crash.

Skirting around the bottom of the car uses the air to increase grip.

The Civic belongs to a breed of racing car designed to satisfy the new rules of the British Touring Car Championship. In order to attract new teams to the competition, a new generation of cars, including the Honda Civic, is being produced that are much cheaper to build and run than before. Even so, it still costs around $300,000 to compete!

Crashes and collisions are common in touring car races so the Civic's fuel tank is protected by Kevlar—the same material that is used in bullet-proof jackets.

There are no creature comforts inside—even the inside door panels have been removed to save weight and reduce the risk of fire.

Although the Civic is a family car, there's no chance of taking the family with you—all the seats, apart from the driver's, have been removed.

SUPER STATS

HONDA CIVIC NGTC
TOP SPEED: 160 mph (257 km/h)
0–60 MPH (0-97 KM/H) : Top secret
HORSEPOWER: Over 300 bhp
LENGTH: Around 177 in (4,500 mm)
WIDTH: Around 70 in (1,770 mm)
HEIGHT: Around 62.9 in (1,600 mm)
MADE IN: Japan

CHEVROLET SS

The Chevrolet SS stands out in America's most popular form of motor sport, NASCAR. These supercars are based on cars that anyone can buy from a showroom. But there's nothing ordinary about the Chevrolet. From its massive engine to its mega-performance, the SS is a thoroughbred racer.

The car is heavier on one side than the other. This is to help the driver deal with the oval-shaped racing tracks with their steeply banked sides.

There are no side windows in the front doors so the driver can get out quickly in the event of an accident.

There have been a number of huge crashes in NASCAR races, so driver safety is important. The Chevrolet has a strong roll cage inside, with an thick extra support beam running through the middle of the car.

Special roof flaps pop up to stop the car from flipping over.

The Chevrolet SS is built to compete in grueling NASCAR races that can last for more 500 miles (800 km). To make it even harder, the races can take place on steeply banked tracks, which puts extra strain on the car and the driver.

Designers spend many hours testing the car in wind tunnels. They make sure air flows around the car properly to give maximum speed and grip.

In the event of an accident, the car is designed to push the engine downward rather than into the driver's legs.

The exhaust pipes are positioned on the right-hand side of the car, away from the driver, who sits on the left.

SUPER STATS

CHEVROLET SS
TOP SPEED: Top secret
0–60 MPH (0-97 KM/H) : Around 5 seconds
HORSEPOWER: Around 415 bhp
LENGTH: 200.4 in (5,090 mm)
WIDTH: 72.9 in (1,852 mm)
HEIGHT: 58.7 in (1,491 mm)
MADE IN: USA

BRISCA STOCK CAR

BriSCA stock cars are the bruisers of the supercar racing world. These near-indestructible race cars are allowed to push and shunt each other out of the way, which leads to real thrill and spill racing. And in stock car racing, the slower cars start at the front so if the fastest drivers want to win, they have to force their way to the front—it's brutal!

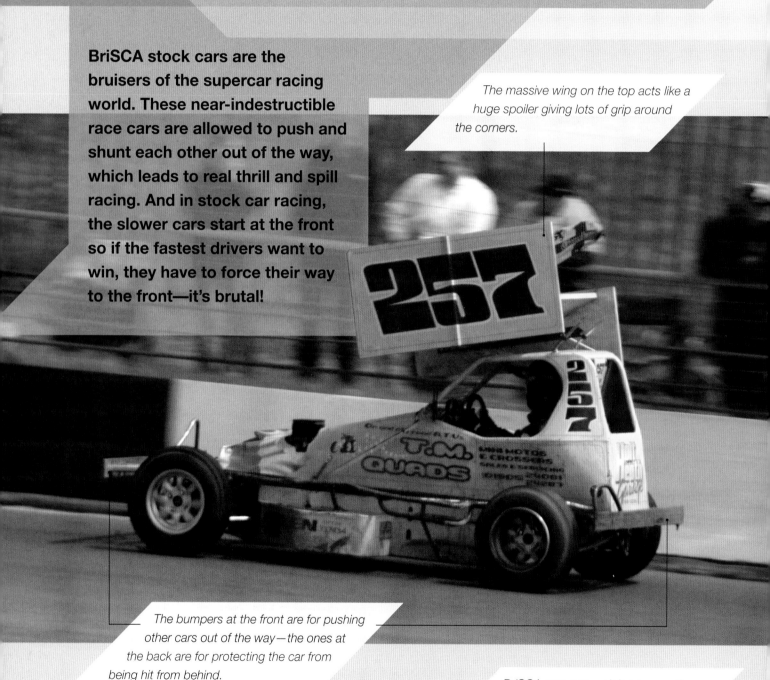

The massive wing on the top acts like a huge spoiler giving lots of grip around the corners.

The bumpers at the front are for pushing other cars out of the way—the ones at the back are for protecting the car from being hit from behind.

BriSCA cars can weigh no more than 3,200 lbs (1,450 kg) and you can have slightly more weight on one side to help it travel round the oval track.

Tires come under lots of pressure during stock car races, so they are made specially for this type of racing.

Not only do these cars have to contend with being bashed around, they also have a tricky race track to race round. Stock cars race around a 400 m (438 yard) oval track, so there's lots of steering involved. Plus, the surface of the tracks can be made of either tarmacadam or a loose gravel-like surface called shale, which offers less grip.

There's no limit to how big the BriSCA's engine can be. Teams have to get the right balance between using the most powerful engine they can without using one that is so heavy that it slows the car down.

Side impact rails offer more protection for the car and driver.

As crashing and bashing is part of the sport, the cars have to be made from high-quality steel tubing to withstand the blows.

SUPER STATS

BRISCA STOCK CAR
TOP SPEED: Around 100 mph (160 km/h)
0–60 MPH (0-97 KM/H) : Around 4 seconds
HORSEPOWER: Around 600 bhp
LENGTH: Around 146 in (3,700 mm)
WIDTH: Around 73 in (1,850 mm)
HEIGHT: Around 54 in (1,370 mm)— not including roof wing
MADE IN: UK

DEMOLITION DERBY

Without a shadow of a doubt, the worst-looking race cars around are those used in action-packed demolition derbies. This wacky group of beaten-up motor cars are having their last hurrah before visiting the scrap heap. And what better way to do it than in an extravaganza of motoring mayhem and destruction!

The original fuel tanks are removed and replaced with smaller, tougher tanks or wrapped in leak-proof material.

A basic roll cage is fitted to protect the driver in the highly likely event that the car gets badly damaged.

For safety reasons the car battery is moved inside the roll cage.

All of the glass and plastic is removed to stop any sharp bits injuring fellow drivers or spectators.

It's against the rules to add any new protective bumpers or to make the body of the car stronger than it was originally. Often bumpers are actually removed.

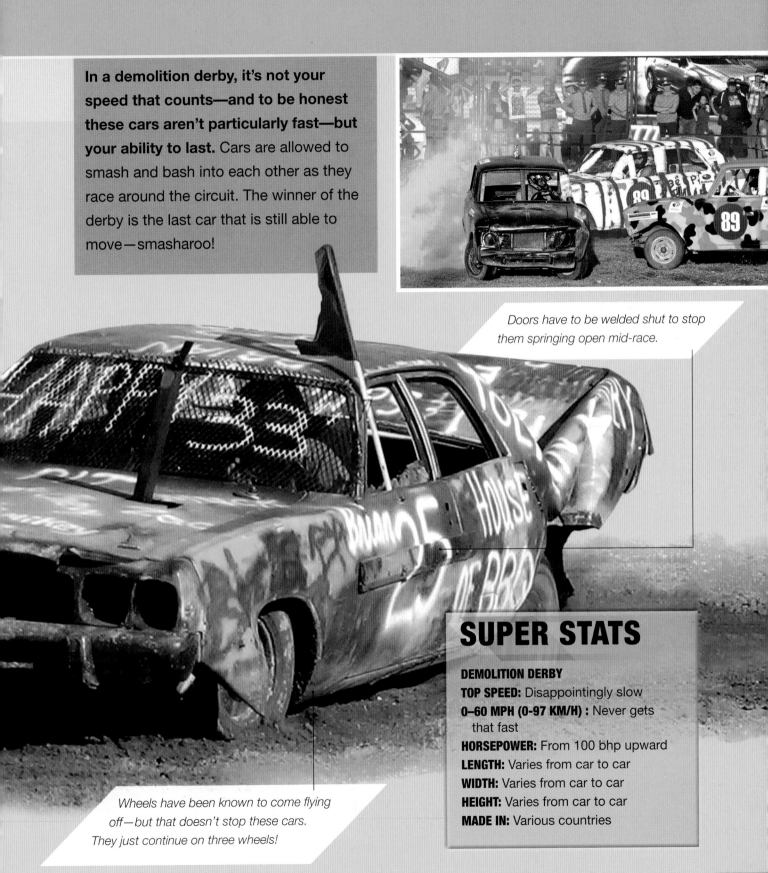

In a demolition derby, it's not your speed that counts—and to be honest these cars aren't particularly fast—but your ability to last. Cars are allowed to smash and bash into each other as they race around the circuit. The winner of the derby is the last car that is still able to move—smasharoo!

Doors have to be welded shut to stop them springing open mid-race.

Wheels have been known to come flying off—but that doesn't stop these cars. They just continue on three wheels!

SUPER STATS

DEMOLITION DERBY
TOP SPEED: Disappointingly slow
0–60 MPH (0-97 KM/H) : Never gets that fast
HORSEPOWER: From 100 bhp upward
LENGTH: Varies from car to car
WIDTH: Varies from car to car
HEIGHT: Varies from car to car
MADE IN: Various countries

MINI ALL4 RACING

The Mini All4 Racing is one of the toughest supercars in the world. This was proved when it won the world's harshest race—the Dakar. To do this, the Mini had to endure all types of harsh driving conditions, from rugged mountains to sweltering deserts, and most of the time the car was off road or following rough tracks. Not only did the Mini do it, but it did it better than anyone else!

The rear seats have been removed, which gives a bigger storage area; handy, as the racers need lots of extra gear—including the three spare tires.

The rear brakes are cooled by jets of water to stop them overheating. If brakes get too hot, they stop working as they should, which would be really bad news!

The tires were specially designed for the Dakar race and have to be tough enough to survive all sorts of different road surfaces.

In 2013 the Mini won the Dakar, a difficult route that went from Peru into Argentina and finished in Chile. The race was more than 5,000 miles (8,000 km) long and lasted for two weeks. Some race days stretched more than 500 miles (800 km). The Mini had to get over the Andes Mountains and survive the Atacama Desert—the driest place on Earth!

The body is made from carbon fiber and is designed so that most parts can be quickly removed and replaced if they get damaged.

Around half the entrants to the Dakar don't finish as the race is so tough on both drivers and their cars.

Unlike most types of race car, the All4 is powered by a diesel engine, which is well-suited for hard, long-distance races such as the Dakar.

The Mini needs as much grip as possible, so the way the air flows over the spoilers is really important as this pushes the car down on to the ground.

SUPER STATS

MINI ALL4 RACING
TOP SPEED: Around 111 mph (178 km/h)
0–60 MPH (0-97 KM/H) : Top secret
HORSEPOWER: 307 bhp
LENGTH: 170.5 in (4,333 mm)
WIDTH: 78.6 in (1,998 mm)
HEIGHT: 78.5 in (1,996 mm)
MADE IN: UK

AUDI R18 E-TRON QUATTRO

The Audi R18 e-tron quattro is arguably one of the most important and impressive racing cars around today. Not only did it win the prestigious Le Mans 24 Hour race, but it achieved this using hybrid technology, proving that part-electric cars can perform as well as—if not better than—normally fueled racers!

The R18 is an endurance racer, which means it takes part in competitions that can last for up to 24 hours. That's tough going for any car.

Every time the Audi driver steps on the brakes, the car stores the energy generated as it slows down. It then uses this energy to power the front wheels.

There are strict rules on how much each racing car can weigh. Having an electric motor and an engine adds weight, so the R18 has a lightweight engine to stop the car being too heavy.

What makes the Audi so special is that it uses a gasoline engine to power the rear wheels and an electric motor to drive the front ones. This hybrid technology is available in family cars, but they tend to be slow and heavy. The R18 has proved that if it's done well it can be a benefit and not a burden!

The wheels are made from magnesium, which is lighter than steel but strong.

The body is made from one single piece of carbon fiber called a monocoque.

Front view cameras increase the driver's view of what's ahead of him by displaying the images in the cockpit.

SUPER STATS

AUDI R18 E-TRON QUATTRO
TOP SPEED: Around 200 mph (320 km/h)
0–60 MPH (0-97 KM/H) : Top secret
HORSEPOWER: Over 490 bhp
LENGTH: 183 in (4,650 mm)
WIDTH: 78.7 in (2,000 mm)
HEIGHT: 40.5 in (1,030 mm)
MADE IN: Germany

CITROËN 2CV

The Citroën 2CV is quite possibly the ultimate racing car. This might sound surprising, as the 2CV hasn't been made for decades. Also, it's slow, has thin wheels and an underpowered engine. However, no other car competes in as many different types of racing as the 2CV. It has taken part in road races, track competitions, rallies, 24-hour races, and even the Dakar!

The 2CV is a very basic car. There are no electric windows, for example—in fact there aren't even wind-up windows! If you want to open the window you have to fold it up!

The body of the car is incredibly light thanks to the thin steel it's made from. This makes it perfect for driving over soft ground.

The 2CV was first made in the 1940s and was designed for people living in the country. The idea was that you could fit a sheep in the back and that the ride would be smooth enough to carry a basket of eggs over a bumpy field without breaking any. No one imagined it was a racing car, but the combination of lightness and excellent suspension made it exactly that!

2CVs don't have a radiator to cool the engine like most cars—instead they use air.

The speedometer on a 2CV only goes up to 70 mph (112 km/h), but it can go faster—especially downhill with the wind behind it.

2CVs are nicknamed "tin snails" thanks to their distinctive shape and less than amazing speeds.

SUPER STATS

CITROËN 2CV
TOP SPEED: Around 90 mph (144 km/h)
0–60 MPH (0–97 KM/H): 35 (yes, thirty-five!) seconds
HORSEPOWER: 29 bhp
LENGTH: 150.7 in (3,828 mm)
WIDTH: 58.2 in (1,478 mm)
HEIGHT: 62.9 in (1,598 mm)
MADE IN: France

SUPER

Superboats are no ordinary boats—they are the fastest, largest, most glamorous, and, often, the werdiest-looking boats you're likely to come across on the open seas!

BOATS

VICTORY TEAM OFFSHORE POWERBOAT

Class 1 offshore powerboats are the Formula 1 cars of the sea. They are designed to streak across water at speeds of more than 107 knots (198 km/h). Victory Team is one of the most successful competitors in this glamorous world. Their boats are really built for speed!

There are two seats inside the cockpit for the driver and "throttleman"—the person in charge of the boat's speed.

Two air intakes at the rear of the boat force air down over the engines to keep them cool.

These boats have two V12 engines—modified versions of the ones used in supercars.

Class 1 powerboat racing is the world's fastest water sport. Boats literally bounce across the seas at incredible speeds. But racing in these vehicles is crazily dangerous. Hitting the water at high speed is like hitting concrete, so the powerboat has to be super-tough. Even so, accidents and even deaths in powerboat racing are not uncommon.

Class 1 boats take a real hammering from the waves at high speed. The hull—the part of the boat in contact with the water—has to be both light and strong. Team Victory's hull is made of carbon fiber and Kevlar, which is also used to make bulletproof vests!

Entry into the cockpit is via a hatch in the roof of the boat.

The boat has two hulls, so it's called a catamaran. Two hulls can be quicker than one, because there is less drag.

SUPER STATS

VICTORY TEAM OFFSHORE POWERBOAT
TO SPEED: 137.6 knots (254.8 km/h)
POWERED BY: Two 8.2-liter V12 engines
ENGINE POWER: 850 hp
LENGTH: 40.6 feet (12.4 m)
WIDTH: 12.3 feet (3.750 m)
WEIGHT: 5.65 tons (4.95 tonnes)
MADE IN: Dubai

RV FLIP

If you're on board a boat and one end starts sinking into the sea, you're usually in big trouble—unless you're on the *FLIP* ship. This unique vessel is designed to tip up so it sticks upright out of the water. Most of the boat is underwater while the bulky bit at the back sits high and dry above the waves. It's all in the name of scientific research.

There is enough room on board for five crew members and 11 scientists—but it's a bit of a tight squeeze!

The furniture on board is attached to the walls with pivots called "trunnions." This means that the furniture spins around the right way up when RV FLIP goes vertical.

It takes about twenty minutes for the ship to go from horizontal to vertical.

The ship's design is based on the shape of a baseball bat—thin at one end and fat at the other.

To make FLIP *tip up*, the crew flood the ballast tanks in the thin part of the hull with water.

People on the boat have to brace themselves against the walls as the ship flips up.

FLIP stands for Floating Instrument Platform, and it's a scientific research vessel. A common problem for scientists studying the sea is that most boats bob up and down, messing up their calculations. That's not true of *RV FLIP*. So much of the ship is below the waves that it stays much more stable, and scientists can make accurate measurements.

FLIP *has no engines, so it has to be towed into its position.*

The scientific equipment is attached to three long arms called booms.

There is a machine on board that makes drinking water, so the crew never runs out—even on long excursions.

SUPER STATS

RV FLIP
MAXIMUM HEIGHT ABOVE WATER LEVEL:
  55 feet (17 m)
TOP SPEED: 7–10 knots
  (13–18.5 km/h) when towed
LENGTH: 354 feet (108 m)
WIDTH: 26 feet (7.93 m)
WEIGHT: 773 tons (711 tonnes)
MADE IN: USA

EARTHRACE / MY ADY GIL

Earthrace—later renamed *MY Ady Gil*—was a strange-looking superboat. However, its weird looks weren't just for show. Its strange fins and narrow hulls were built for a purpose—to make *Earthrace* a record-breaker and the fastest boat ever to sail around the world!

Three thin hulls allowed Earthrace to slice through the waves rather than have to travel over the top of them.

Earthrace was made from carbon and Kevlar, two strong but very light materials.

In 2008 Earthrace broke the record for the fastest boat to travel around the world. It took 60 days, 23 hours, and 49 minutes to make the journey— breaking the old record by 14 hours!

Conditions on the oceans can get pretty rough, so *Earthrace* was designed to survive waves up to 50 feet (15 m) high. It could also go up to 23 feet (7 m) underwater for very short periods.

Water on board the boat was recycled and any other liquids tipped overboard were thoroughly cleaned first.

Not only was *Earthrace* super-fast, it was also kind to the environment. This lean, green speed machine was designed to reuse, recycle or clean as much of the material used onboard as possible. Even the fuels and oils it used came from plants rather than traditional petrol or diesel. *Earthrace* was a superboat with a conscience.

In 2009, *Earthrace* was renamed MY Ady Gil (MY stands for motor yacht) and was used to monitor whale hunting.

In 2010, Ady Gil sank after it collided with a whaling vessel.

SUPER STATS

EARTHRACE / MY ADY GIL
TOP SPEED: 40 knots (74 km/h)
POWERED BY: Two biodiesel engines
ENGINE POWER: 1080 hp
LENGTH: 78 feet (24 m)
WIDTH: 26 feet (8 m)
WEIGHT: 28.7 tons (26 tonnes)
MADE IN: Australia

SPIRIT OF AUSTRALIA

Spirit of Australia is the most "super" of all superboats for one simple reason. It's the fastest boat EVER! If breaking the water speed record weren't a big enough achievement, what made it even more amazing was that *Spirit of Australia* was built in the owner's back yard using everyday tools and secondhand engines.

Spirit of Australia *is called a hydroplane. This type of boat is designed to skim across the top of the water.*

Water slows most boats down. However, hydroplanes are fast because water is forced downward by the bottom of the boat's hull.

The boat is made from timber and sheets of plywood—not the most hi-tech of materials, but clearly good enough!

There's just one seat to keep the weight down.

Spirit of Australia *is powered by a J34 jet engine, normally used in aircraft.*

Ken Warby bought his jet engines from the air force when they were selling off equipment they didn't need.

An Australian named Ken Warby designed, built, and drove *Spirit of Australia* by himself. He had no experience of building a boat like this but had always dreamed of breaking the record and was determined enough to succeed. *Spirit of Australia* broke the record on November 20, 1977. Convinced that his boat could do even better, Warby had another go in October 1978 and broke the record again. That record still stands to this day!

The Australian Royal Air Force helped out by giving the engine an overhaul before the record-breaking attempt.

The official world record was recorded at 317.6 mph (511.11 km/h)—but Spirit of Australia has hit quicker speeds.

SUPER STATS

SPIRIT OF AUSTRALIA
TOP SPEED: Up to 300 knots (555 km/h)
POWERED BY: J34 jet engine
ENGINE POWER: 1,587.6 lbs of thrust
LENGTH: 26.9 feet (8.22 m)
WIDTH: 8.2 feet (2.5 m)
WEIGHT: 1.66 tons (1.5 tonnes)
MADE IN: Australia

ALLURE OF THE SEAS

If biggest is best, then ships don't get any better than *Allure of the Seas*. This is the largest cruise liner in the world! It's like a floating city with shops, a 3-D movie theater, restaurants, a theater, an ice rink, and thousands of people on board. The ship is designed to give passengers the best time possible on the waves.

There is a park in the middle of the ship with 60 trees and thousands of other plants!

The ship has 16 passenger decks.

The bridge sticks out over the side of the hull so the crew can see the edge of the dock when it comes into port.

There are two climbing walls at the back of the ship.

There's even an old-fashioned merry-go-round on board!

At the back of the boat is a gigantic pool. It doubles as an aquatic theater and can spray more than 2,000 jets of water.

Cruise ships are like floating hotels, moving from port to port on grand sightseeing trips. *Allure of the Seas* travels around the Caribbean carrying more than 6,000 passengers. In addition, there are more than 2,000 crew members! You may think it would get crowded. Well, not on this ship—it's huge!

Many people think cruises are for old people. However, on the Allure there's a nightclub just for teenagers, scratch DJ lessons, and an automatic wave machine for surfing.

You need a head for heights—the top of the ship is 213 feet (65 m) above the water line.

SUPER STATS

ALLURE OF THE SEAS

TOP SPEED: 22 knots (41 km/h)
POWERED BY: Four bow thrusters
ENGINE POWER: Four 7,500-hp engines
LENGTH: 1,187 feet (362 m)
WIDTH: 215 feet (66 m)
WEIGHT: 248,711 tons (225,282 tonnes)
MADE IN: Finland

USS GEORGE H. W. BUSH

Aircraft carriers are massive warships that carry thousands of people and equipment for months at a time. The USS *George H. W. Bush* is the biggest warship ever made. If you could stand this ship on end it would be even taller than the Eiffel Tower. It's wider than six telephone poles laid end to end.

Being a warship means that the USS George H. W. Bush could find itself in some pretty dangerous situations. Parts of the ship's hull are protected by Kevlar to prevent damage.

Around 6,000 service personnel and crew live and work on board.

Even the windows have been specially toughened to withstand attack.

The George H. W. Bush usually carries 56 jet planes and 15 helicopters.

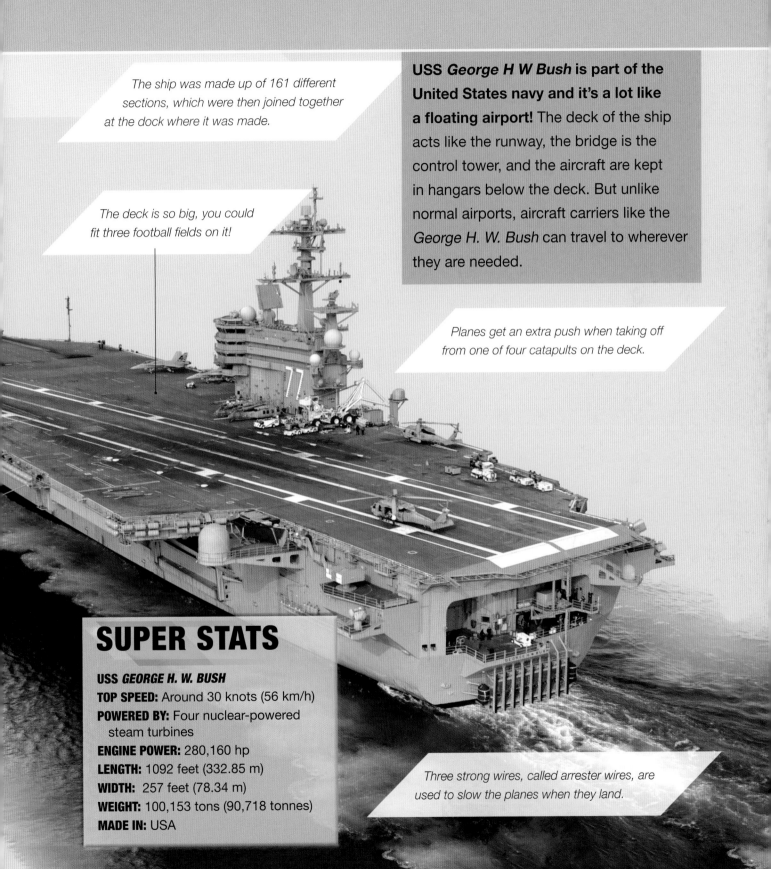

The ship was made up of 161 different sections, which were then joined together at the dock where it was made.

USS *George H W Bush* is part of the United States navy and it's a lot like a floating airport! The deck of the ship acts like the runway, the bridge is the control tower, and the aircraft are kept in hangars below the deck. But unlike normal airports, aircraft carriers like the *George H. W. Bush* can travel to wherever they are needed.

The deck is so big, you could fit three football fields on it!

Planes get an extra push when taking off from one of four catapults on the deck.

SUPER STATS

USS *GEORGE H. W. BUSH*

TOP SPEED: Around 30 knots (56 km/h)

POWERED BY: Four nuclear-powered steam turbines

ENGINE POWER: 280,160 hp

LENGTH: 1092 feet (332.85 m)

WIDTH: 257 feet (78.34 m)

WEIGHT: 100,153 tons (90,718 tonnes)

MADE IN: USA

Three strong wires, called arrester wires, are used to slow the planes when they land.

FRANCISCO

Francisco **may well be the world's most exciting ferry. Most ferries lumber from one dock to another and then back again carrying passengers and usually their vehicles too. Not** *Francisco* **though—this is a super-ferry. It's actually the fastest ship on the water today—even quicker than most speedboats!**

Francisco is classed as a ship rather than a boat because of its large size. However, it is much faster than most smaller crafts.

The ship is powered by two gas turbine engines, usually found on Boeing jet airliners.

Francisco can carry up to 1,024 passengers, plus 150 cars.

Francisco travels across the River Plate from Buenos Aires in Argentina to Montevideo in Uruguay. *Francisco* is so quick that it can compete with airlines over the 140-mile (225-km) distance between the two cities.

The ferry is named for Pope Francis, the head of the Catholic Church.

The catamaran design is used for stability and speed.

The hulls are made from aluminum.

Fuel is stored in the hulls of the ship—each hull provides the fuel for the engine on that side.

FRANCISCO

BUQUEBUS

SUPER STATS

FRANCISCO
TOP SPEED: 58.1 knots (107.6 km/h)
POWERED BY: Two gas turbine engines
ENGINE POWER: 2 x 59,000 hp
LENGTH: 324.8 feet (99 m)
WIDTH: 88.3 feet (26.94 m)
WEIGHT: 497 tons (450 tonnes)
MADE IN: Australia

USA 17

USA 17 was an extreme sailboat designed to race in the 2010 America's Cup. This is one of the oldest yacht races in the world, and pushes both the boats and their crews to their limits. This form of yacht racing demands an extreme superboat—and USA 17 was that boat.

USA 17 was a trimaran, which means it had three hulls.

The three thin hulls were designed to slice through waves.

There were hydrofoils below the hulls to lift the USA 17 out of the water as it traveled, making it even faster.

USA 17 was the fastest yacht ever to win the America's Cup.

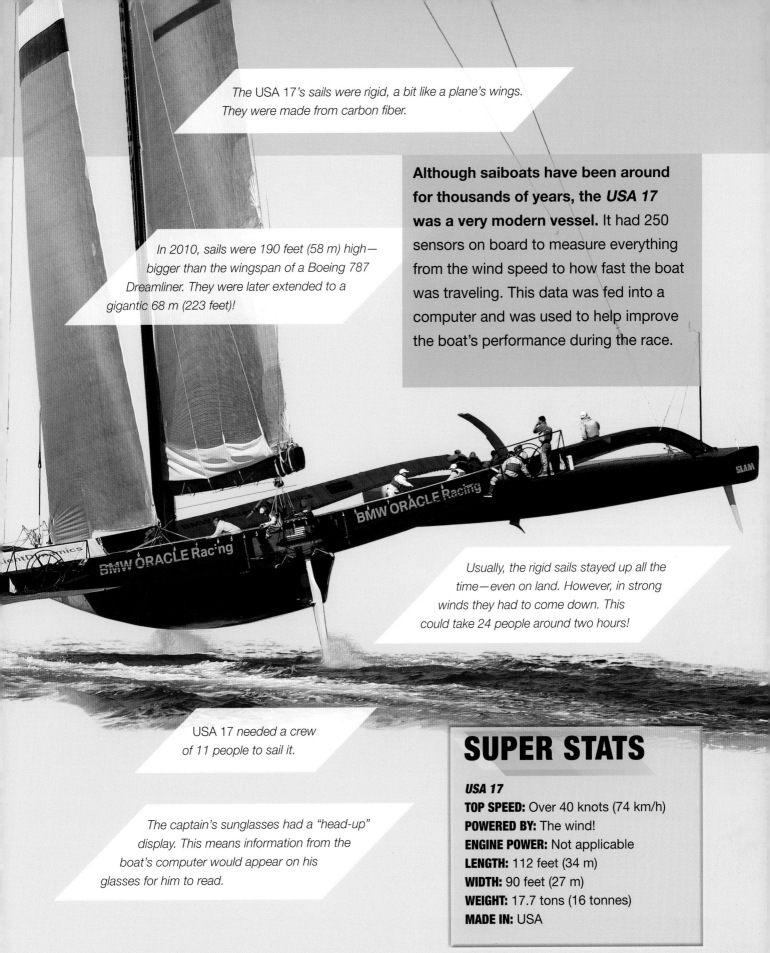

The USA 17's sails were rigid, a bit like a plane's wings. They were made from carbon fiber.

In 2010, sails were 190 feet (58 m) high—bigger than the wingspan of a Boeing 787 Dreamliner. They were later extended to a gigantic 68 m (223 feet)!

Although saiboats have been around for thousands of years, the *USA 17* was a very modern vessel. It had 250 sensors on board to measure everything from the wind speed to how fast the boat was traveling. This data was fed into a computer and was used to help improve the boat's performance during the race.

Usually, the rigid sails stayed up all the time—even on land. However, in strong winds they had to come down. This could take 24 people around two hours!

USA 17 needed a crew of 11 people to sail it.

The captain's sunglasses had a "head-up" display. This means information from the boat's computer would appear on his glasses for him to read.

SUPER STATS

USA 17
TOP SPEED: Over 40 knots (74 km/h)
POWERED BY: The wind!
ENGINE POWER: Not applicable
LENGTH: 112 feet (34 m)
WIDTH: 90 feet (27 m)
WEIGHT: 17.7 tons (16 tonnes)
MADE IN: USA

AV TIGER 12

How many boats can travel over land, water, mud, and even ice? Well, the *AV Tiger 12* can. That's because this superboat doesn't need to touch a surface. It travels over everything on a cushion of air. The *Tiger* is a hovercraft and, thanks to its unique way of getting around, it'll never leave you high and dry!

A motor below the boat blows a layer of air downward. The cushion of air is shaped by a thick rubber "skirt" at the bottom of the boat.

Originally, the Tiger was designed to carry 10 passengers.

There's space for two pilots at the front of the boat.

Rudders at the back of the boat behind the fans are used to steer the Tiger.

The huge fan at the back of the boat isn't for cooling passengers down, but for pushing the Tiger along.

The Tiger is one of the quietest hovercrafts around—which is unusual, because normally hovercrafts are really noisy!

The *Tiger 12* is a very useful kind of superboat. As it doesn't need water to move around, it is ideal for using in places such as mudflats or marshes. That's also why the *Tiger* has been used as a rescue vehicle—no matter where you're stuck, the *Tiger* will probably be able to come and help you!

Hovercrafts can't be used on really rough seas. That's because choppy waves make it too difficult for the "skirt" to keep the layer of air underneath the hovercraft in place.

The tube running around the boat at the top of the "skirt" is always filled with air. This stops the hovercraft sinking if air leaks out from the "skirt."

SUPER STATS

AV TIGER 12
TOP SPEED: 56 knots (104 km/h)
POWERED BY: 5.9 litre V8 engine
ENGINE POWER: 248 hp
LENGTH: 27.9 feet (8.53 m)
WIDTH: 12.5 feet (3.81 m)
WEIGHT: 3.3 tons (3 tonnes)
MADE IN: Great Britain

M/Y A

M/Y usually stands for motor yacht… but this luxury boat is more of a mega yacht! *M/Y A* **took its styling ideas from stealth ships used in navies around the world. This superboat may not be the largest motor yacht on the water, but it is stunningly luxurious and has a unique appearance. If you're rolling in money and want to stand out from the crowd, then this is the boat for you!**

There is a crew of 42 people on board, split between those who sail the boat and those who look after the guests.

There are 14 guest cabins and a master suite.

The hull is made from steel.

A secret room is hidden away inside the boat, just for the owner.

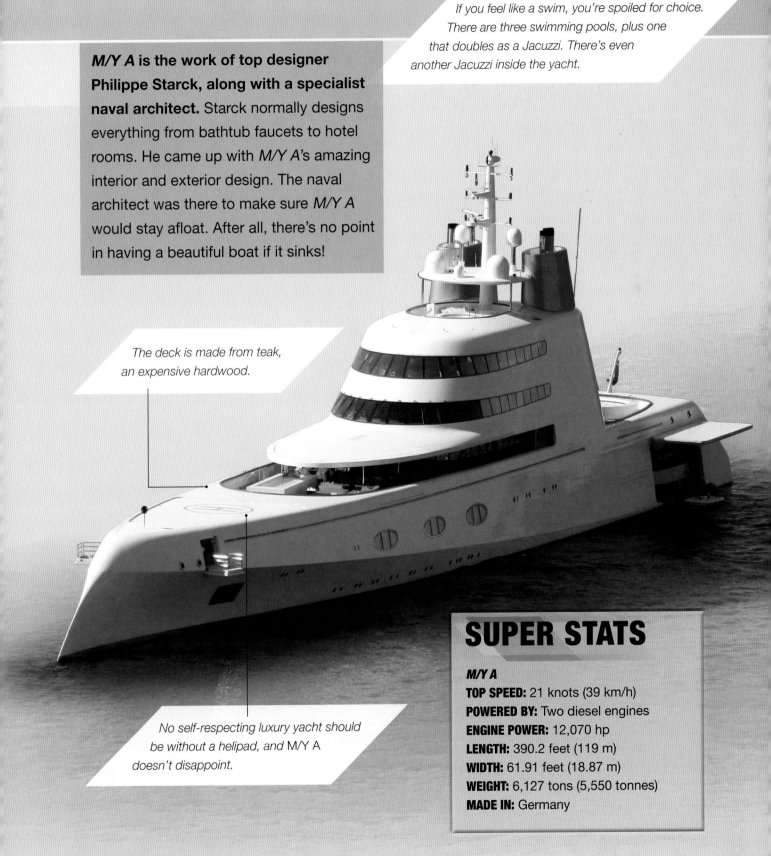

If you feel like a swim, you're spoiled for choice. There are three swimming pools, plus one that doubles as a Jacuzzi. There's even another Jacuzzi inside the yacht.

M/Y A is the work of top designer Philippe Starck, along with a specialist naval architect. Starck normally designs everything from bathtub faucets to hotel rooms. He came up with M/Y A's amazing interior and exterior design. The naval architect was there to make sure M/Y A would stay afloat. After all, there's no point in having a beautiful boat if it sinks!

The deck is made from teak, an expensive hardwood.

No self-respecting luxury yacht should be without a helipad, and M/Y A doesn't disappoint.

SUPER STATS

M/Y A
TOP SPEED: 21 knots (39 km/h)
POWERED BY: Two diesel engines
ENGINE POWER: 12,070 hp
LENGTH: 390.2 feet (119 m)
WIDTH: 61.91 feet (18.87 m)
WEIGHT: 6,127 tons (5,550 tonnes)
MADE IN: Germany

SEA SHADOW

If you spent around $240 million on a ship, wouldn't you want everyone to know about it? That wasn't the case with *Sea Shadow*. This special ship was a stealth craft designed for the US Navy. It used special technology that made it hard to detect—very handy if you're sneaking up on people!

The Sea Shadow's strange shape was deliberate. It made it difficult to detect with the radio waves used by radar.

The special black paint coating the hull also played a part in helping to hide it from radar.

The catamaran design helped the boat to stay stable on the waves.

There was space for 12 bunks on the ship, but there could be twice that number of sailors on board. It wasn't a squeeze, though—while one half of the crew slept the other was on duty.

The hull of the ship was at a 45° angle.

Sea Shadow was a top secret ship. It was never used in a conflict situation. Instead it was used by the US Navy to test out their stealth technologies. This ship was so secret that it was hidden away while it was being built and whenever it wasn't at sea. This, combined with its stealth capacities, made it unlikely that many people ever saw it at all!

For the boat to stay hidden, it was important for the hull to be as smooth as possible, so the doors fitted very snugly into the side.

When the Navy had finished with their testing, Sea Shadow was sold for scrap. It was broken up in 2012! After all the money spent on the boat, the scrap price was just $2.8 million.

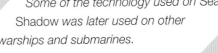

Some of the technology used on Sea Shadow was later used on other warships and submarines.

SUPER STATS

SEA SHADOW
TOP SPEED: 14 knots (26 km/h)
POWERED BY: 2 x diesel electric generators
ENGINE POWER: Top secret
LENGTH: 164 feet (50 m)
WIDTH: 68 feet (20.73 m)
WEIGHT: 618 tons (560 tonnes)
MADE IN: USA

SEABREACHER

Submarines may be exciting vehicles, but they tend to look a little bit... dull. Not *Seabreacher*, though—a super-submersible that can leap through the water like a dolphin and cut through the waves like a shark. Can there be a cooler way of traveling both above and below the water?

There are two seats: the pilot sits up front and the passenger behind.

It would cost you around $100,000 to buy a Seabreacher. That may seem expensive for splashing around in the water—but it's cheap compared to a luxury yacht!

The hull can be painted however the customer likes. Dolphin, shark, or killer whale designs are popular.

The interior of the Seabreacher can also be decorated however the customer chooses.

The _Seabreacher_ isn't a true submarine. For a start, its engine needs air to work and it can't get air underwater. However, the _Seabreacher_ can stay underwater for around a minute, so as long as you are happy to keep surfacing every now and again you'll be fine. It's a lot like being a dolphin!

A snorkel-like vent sends air to the engines.

The canopy is tinted, like sunglasses, to protect the driver and passenger from the sun's rays.

Cameras at the front and rear of the Seabreacher send pictures into the cabin.

SUPER STATS

SEABREACHER X
TOP SPEED: 43.4 knots (80.4 km/h)
POWERED BY: 1,500 cc supercharged engine
ENGINE POWER: 260 hp
LENGTH: 17 feet (5.18 m)
WIDTH: 3 feet (0.9 m)
WEIGHT: 1,350 pounds (612.35 kg)
MADE IN: USA

FSWH 37

The *FSWH 37* is a superboat with a difference—it "flies" across the water on underwater wings! The wings point down instead of pointing out to the side as on an aircraft. The *FSWH*'s wings do the same job as a plane's wings— they lift the boat up. And like a plane, the *FSWH* is super-fast!

The FSWH 37 is used as a passenger ferry—probably for people in a hurry!

The hull is made from lightweight aluminum. This material has the advantages of being strong and resistant to rust.

Underwater, the wings look like upside-down capital letter "T"s.

There's space for 250 passengers on board.

The *FSWH 37* is known as a hydrofoil. That's the name for a boat with wings (called "foils"). A hydrofoil uses its wings to make sure it stays out of the water as much as possible, so that there is less drag from the water. As the *FSWH* accelerates, the wings lift it up and the boat rises out of the water.

FSWH stands for "Fully Submerged Wing Hydrofoil."

Hydrofoils come in different designs. Some have wings that are partly visible on the surface. The main parts of FSWH 37's wings are completely underwater.

SUPER STATS

FSWH 37
TOP SPEED: 43 knots (80 km/h)
POWERED BY: 4 x 16V diesel engines
ENGINE POWER: 3,110 hp
LENGTH: 122.3 feet (37.3 m)
WIDTH: 26.2 feet (8 m)
WEIGHT: 33.1 tons (30 tonnes)
MADE IN: Italy

SKYSAILS

How do you turn an ordinary cargo ship into a vehicle at the cutting edge of green technology? Try adding a high-tech sail! You may have thought that the days of transporting goods on sailing ships were long gone, but think again. The SkySails system fitted to modern cargo ships shows that looking back to the past is the way forward for shipping.

The sail is around 3,445 square feet (320 sq m) in size.

The SkySail is controlled by a computer. It is released, controlled, and finally brought back on board the ship automatically, with very little help from the crew.

The kite flies up to 165 feet (50 m) above the ship.

The towing rope is 1,780 feet (421 m) long.

Ships that use less fuel don't just save money. They also cut back on the pollution in the Earth's atmosphere.

It might look too small to make much difference, but the SkySail can save a lot of fuel. It's also saving the ship owner's money by using the power of the wind to move the ship along. The main difference between the sailing ships of the past and the SkySails system is that these high-tech versions use old ideas in a brand-new way.

The SkySail is designed to help the ship's engines, not replace them.

The cable attaching the kite to the ship is made from a super-strong synthetic fiber. You don't want to lose your kite in the middle of the ocean.

SkySails can save up to 35% of a cargo ship's fuel cost.

SUPER STATS

SKYSAIL CARGO SHIP (THE STATS HERE ARE FOR THE *AGHIA MARINA*)
TOP SPEED: 14 knots (26 km/h)
POWERED BY: One diesel engine and a SkySail
ENGINE POWER: 8,000 hp
LENGTH: 557.7 feet (170 m)
WIDTH: 88.5 feet (27 m)
WEIGHT: 31,488 tons (28,522 tonnes)
SKYSAIL MADE IN: Germany

SUPER

Some of the biggest, speediest, and most expensive copters in the world, these supercopters are amazing flying machines—they can take off vertically and land almost anywhere!

COPTERS

EUROCOPTER X3

Supercopters are the most incredible vertical takeoff vehicles in the world. The Eurocopter X3 may look a little weird—that's because it has more engines and more rotors than most helicopters. This means more power and of course more power equals more speed!

The engines are made by Rolls–Royce, which is a famous luxury car manufacturer.

The X3 is designed as a rapid response helicopter—handy for rescues or for military use.

The X3 is a prototype, which is an experimental vehicle used to test new technology and design.

Short wings keep the forward rotors away from the main body of the helicopter.

X3 broke the unofficial helicopter speed record by hitting 255 knots—which is an amazing 293 mph (472 km/h).

It's not just the number of rotors that makes the X3 so fast—it's the way they are arranged. There is large rotor on top. This allows the helicopter to go straight up and down—or vertical takeoff and landing as it is called. Two rotors at the side work like an airplane's propellers, pulling the helicopter through the air.

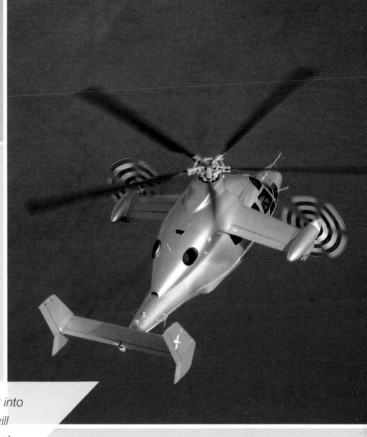

There are no plans to put the X3 into production. Instead, Eurocopter will design a new helicopter based on what it has discovered from the X3.

The two sets of forward facing rotors keep the helicopter stable. They also help it move forward.

SUPER STATS

EUROCOPTER X3

TOP SPEED: 293 mph (472 km/h)
POWERED BY: 2 x Rolls–Royce engines
ENGINE POWER: 2,270 horsepower
CREW: 2
PASSENGERS: 8
MAXIMUM ALTITUDE: 12,500 feet (3,810 m)
MADE IN: France

BELL BOEING V-22 OSPREY

Is it a helicopter or a plane? Actually, it's a supercopter called the V-22 Osprey. The Osprey has a unique way of turning its rotor blades around to get the best of both worlds. It has the vertical lift of a helicopter, plus the straight-line speed and range of a propeller plane. This makes it a really versatile machine that is both useful and quick.

The swiveling engines are known as tiltrotors.

There's space for 9.9 tons (9 tonnes) of cargo inside.

The Osprey is designed to carry either passengers or cargo.

100

Swiveling rotors aren't the only clever bits of technology on the Osprey. This supercopter has been designed so that it can still fly even if one of its engines fails. Helicopters need two sets of rotors to fly. But the Osprey's one good engine can power both sets of rotors to keep the supercopter in the air.

Up to 7.5 tons (6.8 tonnes) of cargo can be carried under the Osprey.

The super-flexible Osprey has proved to be popular with the military.

The wings and rotors can be folded away to make storing the Osprey easier.

SUPER STATS

BELL BOEING V-22 OSPREY
TOP SPEED: 287mph (463 km/h)
POWERED BY: 2 x Rolls–Royce engines
ENGINE POWER: 6,150 horsepower
CREW: Up to 3
PASSENGERS: 24
MAXIMUM ALTITUDE: 25,000 feet (7,620 m)
MADE IN: USA

MIL MI-26 HALO

Supercopters don't get any bigger than the enormous MIL Mi-26 Halo. It's the largest helicopter flying in the skies today. The Mi-26 is a helicopter that was built to carry heavy loads. Thanks to its gigantic size, there are no other helicopters that can do or carry what this supercopter can!

The huge cargo hold measures 39 feet (12 m) long and 10.5 feet (3.2 m) wide.

The Mi-26's massive rotor is 105 feet (32 m) in diameter.

The Mi-26 is useful as a rescue vehicle. It has space for up to sixty stretchers.

The tail skid at the back protects the end of the tail from getting bashed on the ground during takeoff or landing.

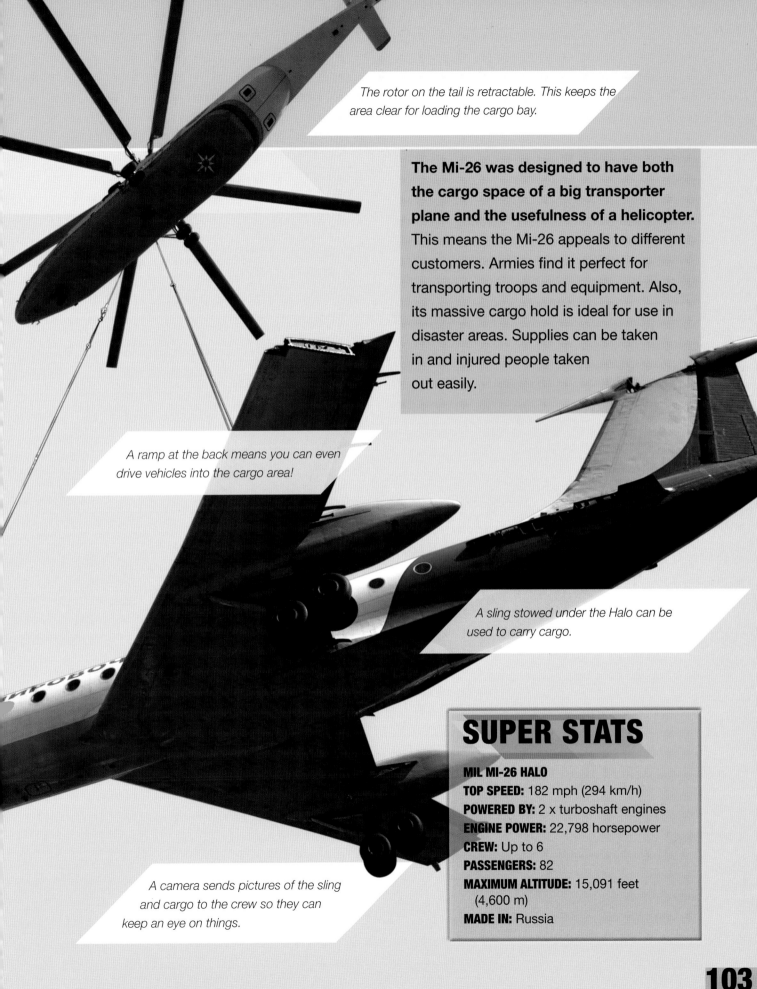

The rotor on the tail is retractable. This keeps the area clear for loading the cargo bay.

The Mi-26 was designed to have both the cargo space of a big transporter plane and the usefulness of a helicopter. This means the Mi-26 appeals to different customers. Armies find it perfect for transporting troops and equipment. Also, its massive cargo hold is ideal for use in disaster areas. Supplies can be taken in and injured people taken out easily.

A ramp at the back means you can even drive vehicles into the cargo area!

A sling stowed under the Halo can be used to carry cargo.

A camera sends pictures of the sling and cargo to the crew so they can keep an eye on things.

SUPER STATS

MIL MI-26 HALO
TOP SPEED: 182 mph (294 km/h)
POWERED BY: 2 x turboshaft engines
ENGINE POWER: 22,798 horsepower
CREW: Up to 6
PASSENGERS: 82
MAXIMUM ALTITUDE: 15,091 feet (4,600 m)
MADE IN: Russia

MOSQUITO AIR

If you think that all helicopters are big, complicated machines, then you've never seen the Mosquito Air! This ultralight vehicle is one of the smallest helicopters in the world. It has so few parts, you'll feel as if you're flying like a bird rather than scooting around in a machine.

The Mosquito Air is made from aluminum tubing and carbon fiber. Both materials are strong but very light.

In some countries, you don't even need a special licence to fly the Air. That's because it's so small and carries so little fuel.

There are other Mosquito helicopters that are similar to the Air. However, these come with a body, windshield, and even floats for landing on water!

Three legs keep the Mosquito Air off the ground.

Although the Air's engine is small, the helicopter is so light that the engine has enough power to get you into the air.

The Mosquito Air was originally designed as a build-it-yourself kit for people to make at home. No specialist knowledge or tools are needed (except some welding equipment). It takes around 200 hours to build the Air. However, for those people without the basic skills—or a welding torch—the company sells ready-made Airs so everyone can enjoy one!

If there were no small rotor at the back of the tail, the helicopter would just spin around and around.

The small metal feet at the ends of the legs are called skid plates.

SUPER STATS

MOSQUITO AIR
TOP SPEED: 69.8 mph (112.6 km/h)
POWERED BY: 1 x two-cylinder engine
ENGINE POWER: 60 horsepower
CREW: 1
PASSENGERS: 0
MAXIMUM ALTITUDE: Around 8,000 feet (2,438 m)
MADE IN: New Zealand

AGUSTAWESTLAND
SEA KING

If you were in trouble at sea or lost on the moors, there's one supercopter you'd want to rescue you—the AgustaWestland Sea King. The Sea King provides 24 hour search and rescue support around Britain. It is equipped with all the technology needed to find and rescue anyone who is in difficulty. In short, the Sea King is a supercopter hero!

A search and rescue Sea King has a crew of four. There are two pilots, plus one person operating the radar and another operating the winch.

There is enough space inside to carry 22 people or nine on stretchers.

The Sea King has an infrared camera that detects body heat.

The infrared camera is useful for finding people when weather conditions make it hard to see.

Sea Kings have been in operation since the 1960s. However, these supercopters are no longer made. Despite this, air forces around the world are still using this model because it's so useful and reliable. Differently equipped Sea Kings are also used to hunt submarines. Others act as mobile early warning systems—that's one super-versatile supercopter!

Pilots wear night-vision goggles to help them fly in the dark.

The Sea King is equipped with a winch for lifting people aboard.

SUPER STATS

AGUSTAWESTLAND SEA KING
TOP SPEED: 144 mph (232 km/h)
POWERED BY: 2 x Rolls–Royce engines
ENGINE POWER: 2,778 horsepower
CREW: 4
PASSENGERS: 22
MAXIMUM ALTITUDE: 10,000 feet (3,048 m)
MADE IN: UK/Italy

BELL HUEY
UH-1H SUPER HUEY

The UH-1H Super Huey might well be the fastest fire engine around. This firefighting supercopter is specially set up to tackle forest fires. These fires are often out of reach to normal fire trucks. Also, they're usually too far away to get to quickly. That's when you need a supercopter like the Super Huey to bring the flames under control and keep people safe.

The Super Huey can carry up to 3,000 lbs (1,360 kg) of weight on the outside.

A winch can be lowered to rescue people on the ground or to attach a stretcher.

The Super Huey has a range of around 250 miles (400 km). That means it can travel 125 miles (200 km) and return home on just one tank of fuel.

The Super Huey can carry a nine-person fire crew. They can then be dropped at the scene of a blaze .

The Super Huey can carry a 340-gallon (1,226 l) bucket of water or firefighting foam. This is hung from below the helicopter and tipped onto the flames.

Although it's brilliant at firefighting, the Super Huey was not designed to tackle forest fires. During the Vietnam War (1959-1975) it was used by the military for a variety of purposes. The Super Huey proved to be such a supercopter that, after the war, lots of surplus helicopters were bought. These were converted to do jobs such as firefighting.

A large tank inside the helicopter can hold up to 368 gallons (1,324 l) of water or foam.

SUPER STATS

BELL HUEY UH-1H SUPER HUEY
TOP SPEED: 138 mph (222 km/h)
POWERED BY: 1 turboshaft engine
ENGINE POWER: 1,800 horsepower
CREW: 1 pilot + 2 fire captains + 8 firefighters
PASSENGERS: 0
MAXIMUM ALTITUDE: Around 19,390 feet (5,900 m)
MADE IN: Dubai

When it isn't fighting fires, the Super Huey can be used for search and rescue missions.

MD902 EXPLORER

The MD902 Explorer is a real crime-fighting supercopter! This versatile helicopter is one of the police's most useful vehicles. It's equipped with all sorts of gadgets specially designed to keep track of criminals down below. The long arm of the law stretches right down from the sky when the Explorer's on duty!

The Explorer doesn't have a tail rotor. Instead, it uses a fan on its tail and air is blown down by the main rotors to keep the helicopter stable. Not having a tail rotor is safer as it means no one can be hit by it.

At night, infrared cameras are used to track criminals. These cameras show body heat rather than a visual image.

Many helicopters suffer from vibration as they hover. Not the MD902. This makes it an ideal supercopter as it can keep a steady position over the action.

A bright searchlight attached to the Explorer is useful for highlighting areas at night.

Chasing criminals can be tricky, but not with this supercopter. Being a helicopter, the Explorer doesn't have to stick to roads. It can hover over the action, keeping an eye on what's going on down below. The crew inside the Explorer is usually made up of a pilot, of course, a police officer, and a paramedic. That means the Explorer can help out in medical emergencies too.

The Explorer keeps in radio communication with police on the ground. That way it can direct them to where they are needed.

The body of the Explorer contains a thin aluminum mesh, which provides protection against lightning strikes.

D-HBWC

Some MD Explorers are also used as air ambulances. The inside can be altered to fit a stretcher too.

SUPER STATS

MD902 EXPLORER
TOP SPEED: 161 mph (259 km/h)
POWERED BY: 2 x Pratt and Whitney engines
ENGINE POWER: 1,100 horsepower
CREW: 2
PASSENGERS: 6
MAXIMUM ALTITUDE: 20,000 feet (6,096 m)
MADE IN: USA

EUROCOPTER EC 135

If you're really rich, then you will need a supercopter to fly you around. It's a great way of getting to the places that private jets can't—like the deck of a luxury yacht. One of the best that you can get is the Eurocopter EC 135. It's light, relatively cheap to run, spacious, and it can be adapted to suit your needs.

The rotor blades sit high above the ground, which stops people being hit by the blades. For added safety, the rear rotors sit inside a covering called a shroud.

Two doors at the back open to reveal a space for luggage.

For a helicopter, the EC 135 is very quiet. This is handy when flying over cities as you don't disturb people.

The EC 135 is also used by some police forces.

EC 135 can carry a satellite telephone on board for making important business calls on the move.

The huge windows give passengers and the pilot an excellent view.

You can arrange the inside of the EC 135 any way that you like. That means it can be used by emergency services around the world as it can fit stretchers inside. However, it really works well as a private aircraft, ferrying business workers from one meeting to another. And the better paid the workers, the more luxurious the EC 135 can be!

D-HVBX

F-HERO

The number of passenger seats can be adjusted depending on the customer. The EC 135 can seat up to seven people comfortably.

SUPER STATS

EUROCOPTER EC 135
TOP SPEED: 161 mph (259 km/h)
POWERED BY: 2 x Pratt and Whitney engines
ENGINE POWER: 816 horsepower
CREW: Up to 2
PASSENGERS: Up to 7
MAXIMUM ALTITUDE: 10,000 feet (3,048 m)
MADE IN: Germany

AGUSTAWESTLAND AW101 VVIP

The AW101 VVIP is a special helicopter for very special people. How special? The clue is in the name—VVIP stands for Very, Very Important Person. Leaders of countries and even royalty choose the AW 101 VVIP as their go-to helicopter. The reason is that it's one of the most luxurious supercopters in the sky.

A weather radar system is installed inside the nose of the AW101. That way the crew knows if bad weather is coming before they can see it.

There are doors to the side and rear.

The cabin is 6 feet (1.83 m) high inside. That might not sound a lot but it's bigger than most private jets.

The AW101 is armor-plated for protection--and the seats can be armor-plated too!

As you might expect with a luxury supercopter, the interior of the AW101 is made to the customer's needs. The type and number of seats inside and how they are laid out are all decisions for the buyer. If you want wardrobes and a shower you can have them—but all this comes at a price. Costs vary according to what is included, but you will need around $19 million if you want to buy one of these luxury supercopters.

Windows can be dimmed electronically, which is handy for both privacy and catching a nap.

External cameras allow passengers and crew to keep an eye on things outside.

The tail is high enough for a limousine to pull right up to the rear doors.

SUPER STATS

AGUSTAWESTLAND AW101 VVIP
TOP SPEED: 172 mph (278 km/h)
POWERED BY: 3 x engines
ENGINE POWER: 7,500 horsepower
CREW: 2
PASSENGERS: Up to 30
MAXIMUM ALTITUDE: 15,000 feet (4,572 m)
MADE IN: UK/Italy

ERIKSON S-64 AIR-CRANE

The S-64's unique looks make it a "one of a kind" type of helicopter. It might look as if it has a big chunk missing out of it but it's been designed that way. The S64 is called an Air-Crane and sometimes a skycrane. Part of its body can be swapped depending on what it is being used for. This supercopter has proved to be useful for both military and civilian purposes.

Since 1992, Air-Cranes have been given names. One of the most famous is called Elvis and works as a firefighting helicopter in Australia.

Air-Cranes have been useful in disaster situations as well as for construction.

The crane can lift can lift about 10 tons (9.1 tonnes)—it's strong enough to carry a helicopter!

The S-64 isn't very fast, but this supercopter was designed for its lifting ability rather than for its speed!

Air-Cranes were originally made by famous helicopter manufacturer Sikorsky. Now they are made by Erickson.

Apart from carrying heavy objects to places that other cranes can't reach, the S-64 is also a versatile supercopter. When it isn't being used as a crane, the helicopter can have attachments fitted underneath it. A pod to carry passengers can be added, or a water tank that turns it into a firefighting machine.

At the back of the cockpit, a rear-facing seat is used by one of the crew to operate the grappling hook.

A strong grapple hangs from the middle of the S-64 for carrying heavy objects.

SUPER STATS

ERIKSON S-64 AIR-CRANE
TOP SPEED: 132 mph (213 km/h)
POWERED BY: 2 x Prat and Whitney engines
ENGINE POWER: 9,000 horsepower
CREW: 3
PASSENGERS: 2
MAXIMUM ALTITUDE: 31,480 feet (9,595 m)
MADE IN: Dubai

BOEING CH-47 CHINOOK

With its twin rotor blades, the Chinook is probably the most easily recognizable helicopter in the world. For more than fifty years, this supercopter has been used both by the military and by civilian companies. That's because this amazing helicopter has proved itself to be both super-reliable and very versatile.

There are three cargo hooks below the Chinook for attaching external cargo.

The Chinook is a record-breaker: no other Boeing helicopter has been in continuous production for so long.

The two sets of propellers are called "tandem rotors."

The tandem rotor system means the Chinook can fly in conditions that may be too extreme for other helicopters.

The Chinook can carry cargo weighing over 9.4 tons (8.5 tonnes).

The Chinook was first introduced in 1962 and is called a multi-mission helicopter. That means it's pretty good at doing virtually everything. It can carry people and it can be used to transport goods. This supercopter can even carry loads suspended from it on straps. This makes it useful in all sorts of places—from war zones and disaster areas to hard-to-reach oil rigs.

There are infrared searchlights on board. This is helpful for finding people at night.

The Chinook was designed for the US military, but it is now used by armed forces across the globe.

SUPER STATS

BOEING CH-47 CHINOOK
TOP SPEED: 184 mph (296 km/h)
POWERED BY: 2 x turboshaft engines
ENGINE POWER: 6,296 horsepower
CREW: 4
PASSENGERS: Up to 44
MAXIMUM ALTITUDE: 4,572 m
  (15,000 feet)
MADE IN: USA

MBB BO-105

Since the early days of the 20th century, watching planes do aerobatics, or stunts in the air, has been popular. But no one thought that doing a loop-the-loop in a helicopter was possible. That's until the MBB BO-105 came along! This agile aircraft is the top choice of helicopter for pilots who want to do aerobatics. This supercopter has responsive controls and a stable flying ability.

Unlike many helicopters, the BO-105 has what is called a rigid rotor system. This means the rotor blades are bolted straight to the rotor head at the top and not fixed to hinges. This is what makes this helicopter ideal for stunts.

Smoke canisters can be attached to the skids during displays.

In an aerobatic display, it's important to see what's around you. The BO-105's huge windows provide excellent visibility.

Originally, the MBB BO-105 wasn't designed for doing stunts. It was built as a multi-purpose helicopter and is used for a variety of very different jobs. Air forces strap missiles to the side of it and use it to destroy tanks. Construction companies use it to carry goods. Medical teams use it for emergencies. But in the hands of a skilled pilot, the BO-105 can really put on a display at an air show!

The rotor head (the part anchoring the rotor blades) is made from titanium, a light but very tough metal.

Aerobatics put a huge strain on the helicopter, so it has a specially strengthened frame to cope with all the difficult stunts.

The rotor blade edges are lined with aluminum to make them stronger.

The lightweight BO-105 is a real pleasure to fly.

SUPER STATS

MBB BO-105
TOP SPEED: 151 mph (243 km/h)
POWERED BY: 2 x turboshaft engines
ENGINE POWER: 860 horsepower
CREW: 1
PASSENGERS: 4
MAXIMUM ALTITUDE: 10,000 feet (3,050 m)
MADE IN: Germany

BOEING SIKORSKY RAH-66 COMANCHE

The best type of defense is not to be spotted in the first place. That's why the RAH-66 Comanche was such a fantastic supercopter. It was designed to be hard to see, hard to hear, and even hard to spot on radar. If you couldn't see it coming, it would have been very hard to shoot it down. This was great news for the pilots on board!

A bulletproof outer body offered excellent protection for the pilots.

Its strange shape made it difficult to spot on enemy radar machines.

Different sorts of missiles could be loaded onto the Comanche. This made it as good at fighting as it was at hiding.

There's a reason why you won't have seen a Comanche helicopter and it's not just due to its clever technology. The Comanche never actually made it into production. Only a couple of prototypes were made, which makes this helicopter super-rare and super-stealthy. However, you can be sure that some of the technology they tried out first on the Comanche is being used on other top-secret stealth helicopters.

The Comanche was much quieter than normal helicopters thanks to the design of the main and tail rotors.

We don't know what the Comanche was made from—it's top secret! This material helped it hide from detection by radar.

The cockpit was sealed so the pilots couldn't be affected by chemical or biological weapons.

The Comanche was in development for around 22 years and is estimated to have cost about $4.5 billion!

SUPER STATS

BOEING SIKORSKY RAH-66 COMANCHE
TOP SPEED: 200 mph (324 km/h)
POWERED BY: 2 x turboshaft engines
ENGINE POWER: 2,864 horsepower
CREW: 2
PASSENGERS: 0
MAXIMUM ALTITUDE: Unknown
MADE IN: USA

SUPERCOPTERS
KAMAN K-MAX UAS

Helicopters need at least one and sometimes two pilots to fly them. That's not true of the K-Max UAS, though. This remarkable machine doesn't need any pilots at all! It isn't as though the K-Max is a tiny remote-control toy. Actually, it's a full-sized helicopter designed for carrying heavy loads!

The K-Max UAS is adapted from the K-Max helicopter, which is a single-seat aircraft.

An operator sends instructions to the K-Max UAS via a laptop computer.

The K-Max doesn't have a tail rotor. Instead, it uses two main rotors turning in opposite directions. This is called a synchropter.

Synchropters are good at hovering—handy for landing cargo on the ground.

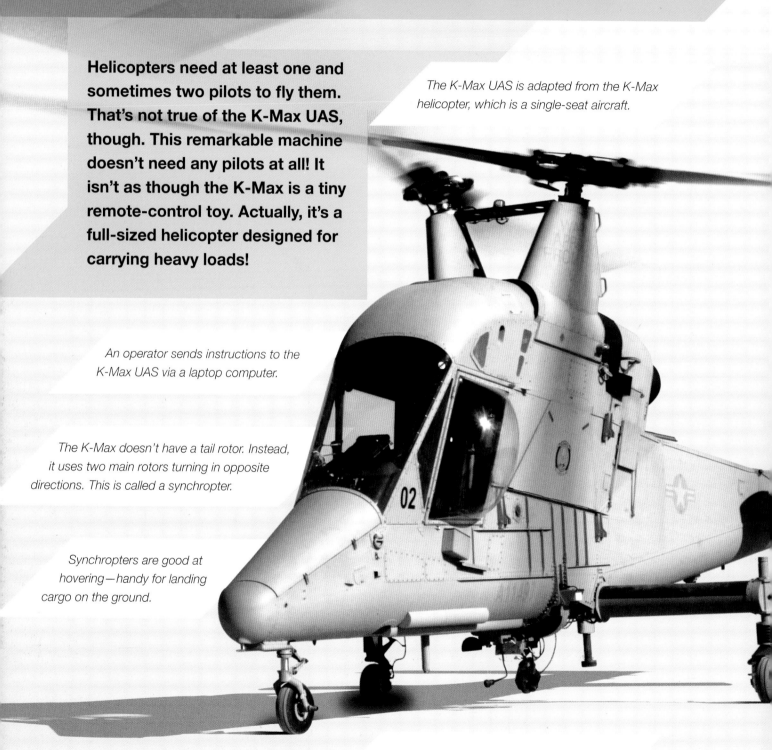

UAS stands for Unmanned Aerial System.

It goes without saying that battlefields are very dangerous places. Therefore, the best way to stay out of danger is not to be there in the first place. That's where the K-Max UAS comes in handy. The K-Max UAS is used to drop supplies in some of the most dangerous places in the world. It does this without having to risk the life of a pilot.

Cargo can be moved automatically along the helicopter's underside to keep it properly balanced.

There's a pilot's seat in the K-Max UAS, so the helicopter can still be flown in the traditional way.

Cargo is carried on four hooks below the helicopter.

SUPER STATS

KAMAN K-MAX UAS
TOP SPEED: 115 mph (185 km/h)
POWERED BY: 1 x gas turbine engines
ENGINE POWER: 1,800 horsepower
CREW: 0 (but there is room for 1)
PASSENGERS: 0
MAXIMUM ALTITUDE: 29,117 feet (8,875 m)
MADE IN: USA

GLOSSARY

ABS This stands for "Anti-lock Braking System," which slows cars down safely.

aerobatics Stunts performed by an aircraft.

aerodynamic Designed to move through the air easily.

air scoop An opening in the car's hood that enables air to flow in and cool the engine.

altitude The height of an object compared to sea or ground level.

aluminum A lightweight metal.

ballast tank An area within a boat that holds water and helps the ship float.

bhp This stands for "brake horsepower," and is a measurement of the engine's power.

carbon fiber A strong, light material made from thin rods of carbon. Carbon is also found in coal and diamonds.

catamaran A ship with two parallel hulls.

chassis The base of a motor vehicle.

cockpit The space in a car, plane, boat, or helicopter where the driver sits.

cowling A metal covering that protects the engine of a vehicle.

eco-friendly Not harmful to the environment

fiberglass A covering material that is made from glass fibers.

friction A force that resists motion between two objects.

hovercraft A vehicle with an air-cushion that can travel on both land and water.

hybrid car A car that uses two or more power sources.

hydrofoil A boat that has fins, allowing it to lift off the water and travel at faster speeds.

infrared A color of light that cannot be seen by human eyes. Infrared radiation can be detected by cameras and search lights as heat.

Kevlar A man-made material that is very strong and resistant to heat.

knots A way of measuring the speed of aircraft and boats. 1 knot is equal to approximately 1.151 mph (1.852 km/h).

magnesium alloy A mixture of magnesium and other metals.

mpg This stands for "miles per gallon." It means the distance a car can travel using one gallon of fuel.

nitromethane An organic compound used as a racing fuel in Top Fuel drag racing.

performance figures Measurements that show how well a car works.

plywood A strong type of board, made by gluing two or more layers of wood together.

radar A means of detecting objects using radio waves.

roll cage A frame built into the passenger compartment in a vehicle to protect the occupants from being injured in a crash.

rotor A group of blades on a helicopter that rotate to lift the vehicle.

satellite An object that travels around a planet in a regular orbit.

spoiler A device fitted to the rear of a vehicle, designed to help improve the airflow over the car and increase its speed.

submersible A boat that can go underwater.

surplus More than what is needed.

synchropter A helicopter with two main rotors that turn in different directions.

titanium A shiny white metal that does not rust easily.

trimaran A ship with three parallel hulls.

trunnion A pin or pivot on which an object can be rotated.

tubular Long, round and hollow; shaped like a tube.

turbine engine A type of engine in which a wheel is turned by water, gas, or steam to create continuous power.

winch A machine with a rope or chain that is used for lifting or pulling objects.

PICTURE CREDITS

AgustaWestland: 97, 114b, 114–115c, 115t. Ahmed Jadallah/Reuters/Corbis:68bl. Ariel Ltd: contents, back cover bl, 7bl, 34, 35. Audi UK: cover, 36, 62–63. Automobili Lamborghini: 12, 13. Boeing: 2, 96, 122–123c. Bradhall71: 50b. Carlo Borlenghi/Alinghi/NewSport/Corbis:82tr. Corbis: 106bl (David Billinge/Demotix), 28 (Car Culture), 29 (Car Culture), 106–107c (Jim Orr / Demotix/Demotix), 107tr (George Hall), 108 (Kent Porter/ZUMA Pres), 64 (HOCH ZWEI/Thomas Suer/dpa), 103c (ANATOLY MALTSEV/epa), 48 (Transtock), 102c (Wojtek Lembryk/epa), 109 (Randy Pench/ZUMA Press). Crystal/Splash News/Corbis: 87. ED Archives: 1, 18, 19. Eurocopter: back cover tl, 5b, 98–99c, 99t, 112c, 113t, 113b. Ford of Britain: back cover br, 6, 32, 33. General Motors: 36, 54, 55. Getty: 24–25. Gsenkow: 3, 40–41. Hovercraft Rentals, Orpington, UK: 84, 85. IFCAR: 9tr. Morgan Motor Co: 16–17. Incat/Buquebus Marketing: 80, 81. Innespace Productions Inc: back cover tr, 90–91. Intermarine SpA, Messina, Italy: cover 92, 93. Juergen Lehle (albspotter.eu): 110–111. Limeydal: 83. Noble Automotive Ltd: cover cr, 26–27, 22t, 22b. OSX: 3, 8–9. PCN/Corbis: 82bl. Porsche Cars Great Britain: 10–11. Regular Daddy: 116–117c. Royal Caribbean Cruises Ltd: 66, 67t, 76, 77. Shutterstock: 24b (Angyalosi Beata), 69tr (Geanina Bechea), 20c, 21 (Dongliu), 20b (Gustavo Fadel), 36, 44–45, 60 (Rodrigo Garrido), 68–69 c (Iliuta Goean), 59tr (Art Konovalov), 53, 65 (Luis Louro), 52 (Julie Lucht), 120 and 121 (Anatoliy Lukich). 58–59 (Jason Meredith), cover c, 14–15 (Sam Moores), 4b, 38–39 (Natursports), 56–57 (Martin Preston), 42–43 (PhotoStock10), 46–47 (Philip Rubino), 61 (Christian Vinces). SkySails GmbH: 94, 95. Spyker Cars/The S3 Agency: 30–31. Ted Soqui/Corbis: 3b, 86. Transtock/SuperStock: 49. UNSW Solar Car Racing Team—Sunswift: 37, 50t, 51. U.S. Air Force photo: 3l, 97t, 100t and 101c (Senior airman Julianne Showalter), 119t (Staff Sgt. Thomas Trower), 119b (Senior Airman Steven R. Doty). U.S. Army photo: 118. USDOD: 117t. US Marine Corp: 96, 124. US National Archives: 125. U.S. Navy: 70t (John F. Williams), 70b (John F. Williams), 71 (John F. Williams), 78l (Mass Communication Specialist 2nd Class Samantha Thorpe), 78br (courtesy of Northrop Grumman by Alan Radecki), 67, 79 c (Mass Communication Specialist 2nd Class Michael Smevog), 88 (courtesy of Naval Sea Systems Command), 89tr (Photographer's Mate 2nd Class Sheldon Archie), 89bl (Courtesy of Lockheed Martin). Warby Motorsport: 4t, 74, 75.